T0312296

Cambridge Elements ≡

Elements on Women in the History of Philosophy
edited by
Jacqueline Broad
Monash University

LUCREZIA MARINELLA

Marguerite Deslauriers
McGill University

CAMBRIDGE
UNIVERSITY PRESS

Shaftesbury Road, Cambridge CB2 8EA, United Kingdom

One Liberty Plaza, 20th Floor, New York, NY 10006, USA

477 Williamstown Road, Port Melbourne, VIC 3207, Australia

314–321, 3rd Floor, Plot 3, Splendor Forum, Jasola District Centre, New Delhi – 110025, India

103 Penang Road, #05–06/07, Visioncrest Commercial, Singapore 238467

Cambridge University Press is part of Cambridge University Press & Assessment, a department of the University of Cambridge.

We share the University's mission to contribute to society through the pursuit of education, learning and research at the highest international levels of excellence.

www.cambridge.org

Information on this title: www.cambridge.org/9781009479349

DOI: 10.1017/9781009029162

First published 2024

A catalogue record for this publication is available from the British Library.

ISBN 978-1-009-47934-9 Hardback
ISBN 978-1-009-01401-4 Paperback
ISSN 2634-4645 (online)
ISSN 2634-4637 (print)

Lucrezia Marinella

Elements on Women in the History of Philosophy

DOI: 10.1017/9781009029162
First published online: March 2024

Marguerite Deslauriers
McGill University

Author for correspondence: Marguerite Deslauriers,
marguerite.deslauriers@mcgill.ca

Abstract: Lucrezia Marinella's (1571–1653) most important contributions to philosophy were two polemical treatises: *The Nobility and Excellence of Women, and The Defects and Vices of Men,* and the *Exhortations to Women and to Others if They Please.* Marinella argues for the superiority of women over men in every respect: psychologically, physiologically, morally, and intellectually. She is particularly effective in using the resources of ancient philosophy to support her various arguments, in which she draws conclusions about the souls and the bodies of women, the nature and significance of women's beauty, the virtue of women, and the liberty to which women as well as men are entitled. This Element showcases that her claim of superiority is intended ultimately to justify the possibility of political rule by women.

Keywords: Lucrezia Marinella, Renaissance feminism, superiority and equality, beauty, liberty

ISBNs: 9781009479349 (HB), 9781009014014 (PB), 9781009029162 (OC)
ISSNs: 2634-4645 (online), 2634-4637 (print)

Contents

1 Introduction

On December 27, 1595, Lucrezia Marinella wrote a letter from Venice to the Duchess of Ferrara, Margherita Gonzaga. A month earlier she had sent the Duchess a copy of her first book, newly published, *La Colomba sacra, poema heroico* (*The Sacred Dove*), through an intermediary. After setting out that fact, Marinella writes:

> not having to date received any response I am surprised, and suspect one of
> two causes: either Your Highness was not pleased with the gift, or else Your
> Highness did write to me, and the letter has gone astray. However that may be,
> let Your Highness favour me, if she should consider me unworthy of her
> grace, at least by consoling me with one of her letters. That would give me
> heart to write poetry more happily. I wish to receive a response from you even
> more because I am often beset by this or that gentlewoman who asks me what
> response I have had from you.

Marinella was young, without an established reputation, but the tone of the letter is remarkably confident. She makes clear that she expects a reply, even if the book is not to the liking of the Duchess, and that the knowledge of the Duchess's displeasure would not stop her writing. The letter also reveals that Marinella had informed her acquaintance (the "gentlewomen") that she had sent a copy of *La Colomba sacra* to the Duchess, which suggests that she was open about her literary aspirations. The letter is polite and is signed "a devoted servant of Your Highness," but it is remarkably unfawning (particularly when compared with contemporary letters to the Duchess by male courtiers), without the customary inflated praise offered by someone seeking patronage. It reveals something of Marinella's character: the ambition, the confidence, the willingness to promote her work, the commitment to a writing career, and – if only implicitly – the appreciation of political power wielded by a woman. It was effective: on January 10, 1596, the Duchess sent a response through her secretary, enclosing "a small gift" that Marinella, in her reply of January 17, says she will keep with her "unto the dark tomb."[1]

2 Life and Works

2.1 Life

Lucrezia Marinella was born into a family of *cittadini* (citizens), "a peculiarly Venetian status category standing between the ruling patriciate and the *popolo* [people]" who were "excluded from holding political office but otherwise comparable to the lower ranks of the patriciate in terms of wealth, education,

---

[1] The original exchange of letters is in the Archivio di Stato di Modena, Archivio Segreto Estense Cancelleria, Archivio per materie, Letterati Busta 34, Fasc. 28.

and social prestige."[2] Her status as a *cittadina* allowed her to pursue her intellectual career; had she been a member of the "*popolo*" she would not have had the education or the liberty necessary to write and publish, and had she been patrician it would have been considered inappropriate for her to do so.

Of Marinella's mother no record survives. Her father, Giovanni Marinelli, was a physician, who published a number of medical works, two of which concerned women. They were written in the vernacular, which suggests that he intended them to be read by women; one was a guide to hygiene and beauty, the other a work on the illnesses of women.[3] Marinella's brother Curzio was also a physician who wrote medical treatises and commented on two historical works, which showed him to be a proponent "of a Machiavellian, aristocratic republicanism," popular in Venice in that period.[4] The family context thus embraced literary pursuits, a knowledge of natural philosophy and medicine, and an aristocratic republicanism, all of which had a bearing on Marinella's work.

There is conflicting evidence on the date of Marinella's birth in Venice, which was either in 1571 or in 1579.[5] In 1607 Marinella married another physician, Girolomo Vacca, with whom she had two children, Antonio and Paolina. Since her husband's family was property-owning and well-connected, it is likely that her marriage raised her status somewhat and placed her in a wider social milieu.[6] Marinella had lived in Venice until her marriage, and returned there with Vacca after some years in Padua. When her husband died in 1629, Marinella remained in Venice, where, as a *cittadina* and a widow, she was able to act on behalf of her family in legal and financial transactions.[7] Her primary political loyalty was to Venice – she declared herself to be "*suddita*"

---

[2] V. Cox, *Women's Writing in Italy* (Baltimore: The Johns Hopkins University Press, 2008), p. 5; V. Cox, *The Prodigious Muse: Women's Writing in Counter-Reformation Italy* (Baltimore: The Johns Hopkins University Press, 2011), p. 5.

[3] *Gli ornamenti delle donne* (1562) and *Le medicine partenenti alle infirmità delle donne* (1563, rev. 1574). On Giovanni Marinelli, see F. Lavocat, "Introduzione," in L. Marinella, *Arcadia felice* (Florence: Olschki, 1998), p. xi.

[4] Lavocat, "Introduzione," p. xii.

[5] According to the record of her death in the church of San Pantalon in Venice, Marinella was eighty-two, which would have made her year of birth 1571; S. Haskins, "A Portrait," in A. Cagnolati (ed.), *A Portrait of a Renaissance Feminist: Lucrezia Marinella's Life and Works* (Rome: Aracne, 2013), pp. 13–14. But a portrait of Marinella painted in 1601 had a legend saying that she was twenty-two in that year, which would suggest, alternatively, that 1579 was the year of her birth; Haskins, "A Portrait," p. 12, n. 3; L. Benedetti, "Le *Essortationi* di Lucrezia Marinella: l'ultimo messaggio di una misteriosa Veneziana," *Italica*, 85:4 (2008), 393, n. 12. For the most comprehensive account of the facts of Marinella's life, based on notarial documents, see S. Haskins, "Vexatious Litigant, or the Case of Lucrezia Marinella? New Documents Concerning her Life (Part I)," *Nouvelles de la République des Lettres* 1 (2006), 80–128, and "(Part II)," *Nouvelles de la République des Lettres* 1–2 (2007), 203–230.

[6] Haskins, "A Portrait," p. 30.   [7] Haskins, "A Portrait," p. 33.

(subject) to the Republic of Venice in the dedication of *La vita di Maria Vergine imperatrice dell'universo* (*The Life of the Virgin Mary, Empress of the Universe*) to the Doges of Venice in 1602.[8] But she also implies an ongoing connection with Modena in a letter to the Duchess of Ferrara in that same year, written to accompany a copy of the same work, by saying that her father was born in Modena, and that she wished to be "*Suddita*" to the Duchess.[9] She died of quartan fever (malaria) in 1653, at the age of eighty-two.[10]

If Marinella's social class was one factor in making possible her literary career, her education was another. There is little documentary evidence of that education, but in dynastic families in the courts of northern Italy in the sixteenth century it was usual to educate women, and in some cases the aspirations of Venetian *cittadini* to emulate the patrician class may have motivated fathers to educate their daughters. Among humanists generally the literary and philosophical cultivation of daughters could be seen as a flattering reflection of their own education.[11] It is reasonable to assume that Marinella had access to her father's and eventually her husband's libraries, and that the knowledge of moral and natural philosophy, as well as literature, that she demonstrates in her work was obtained at home. Her references to Aristotle suggest a direct acquaintance with the Latin translations of some of his works, and she may have had instruction in that language.[12]

Marinella's intellectual connections extended beyond her family. She interacted with members of the second Accademia Veneziana, one of whom, Lucio Scarano, was its secretary and the dedicatee of her polemic *La nobiltà et l'eccellenza delle donne, co' diffetti et mancamenti de gli huomini* (*The Nobility and Excellence of Women, with the Defects and Vices of Men*) (Venice: Giovanni Battista Ciotti, 1601).[13] Boncio Leone, the author of a sonnet in praise of Marinella appended to *La Colomba sacra*, was the founder

---

[8] Lavocat, "Introduzione," p. xv.

[9] The Duchess was Virginia de' Medici, wife of Cesare d'Este (Haskins, "A Portrait," p. 13). The letter is in the Biblioteca Estense Universitaria in Modena (α.G.1.16 [54]).

[10] On the cause of Marinella's death, see Haskins, "A Portrait," pp. 33–34.

[11] Cox, *Women's Writing*, p. 6 and p. 262, n. 23, where Cox mentions Marinella as an example of this trend. For an excellent overview of humanism, see Margaret L. King, "A Return to the Ancient World?" in *The Oxford Handbook of Early Modern European History* (Oxford: Oxford University Press, 2015), pp. 3–28. On the difficulties women encountered in obtaining an education in the century prior to Marinella, see Margaret L. King, "Six Learned Women of the Italian Renaissance," *Soundings: An Interdisciplinary Journal* 59:3 (Fall 1976), 280–304.

[12] See L. Marinella, *Exhortations to Women and to Others if They Please*, L. Benedetti (ed., trans., and intro.) (Toronto: Centre for Reformation and Renaissance Studies, 2012), p. 38, p. 161, n. 299; see also S. G. Ross, *The Birth of Feminism: Woman as Intellect in Renaissance Italy and England* (Cambridge, MA: Harvard University Press, 2009), p. 202.

[13] I refer to the Italian text as *La nobiltà* or *Nobiltà*; when citing the English translation by Dunhill, I refer to '*Nobility*'. Lavocat, "Introduzione," p. xiv; Cox, *Women's Writing*, p. 322, n. 3; S. Kolsky, "Moderata Fonte, Lucrezia Marinella, Giuseppe Passi: An Early Seventeenth-Century Feminist Controversy," *The Modern Language Review*, 96:4 (2001), 975–977.

and president of the Accademia Veneziana.[14] The publisher of many of her works, Giovanni Battista Ciotti, was publisher to the Accademia; since Ciotti seems to have commissioned the *Nobiltà*, Marinella may have been writing her defense of women as a "semi-authorized spokeswoman for the academy"; certainly she had a "distanced but productive" relationship with the academy.[15] Many other of Marinella's dedicatees were women with some power at the courts of northern Italian cities (e.g., the duchesses of Mantua and Ferrara).[16] In dedicating her works to these women she may have hoped both to obtain cultural patronage and to reach a wider public among women.

The first of her works to be published, *La Colomba sacra*, appeared in 1595; her last work, *Holocausto d'amore della vergine Santa Giustina* (*The Inferno of Love of the Virgin Saint Justine*), was published in 1648. Between 1595 and her marriage in 1607, Marinella published nine books; nothing more from her appeared in print until 1624, when her biography of Saint Catherine of Siena was published, followed by several more works in a variety of genres until a few years before her death. To explain the hiatus in Marinella's publishing career, most scholars assume that during the period between 1607 and 1624 she was occupied with child-bearing and rearing.[17] One speculates that "the silence may have been due to the reception of *La Vita di Maria* [*Vergine*]" – but Marinella published three more works after it and before her marriage.[18] Another suggests a link between the demise of the second Accademia Veneziana around 1609 and this period of silence from Marinella.[19] What is clear is that Marinella wrote and published in every phase of her life: before marriage, in the later years of her marriage, and in widowhood. Neither youth, nor age, nor domestic duties suppressed her intellectual activity for long.

2.2 Works

Marinella wrote in Italian, sometimes quoting from Latin sources. Her oeuvre is remarkable for its extent, for the variety of genres in which she wrote, and for her interest in moral and natural philosophy.[20] Many of her works, including the

---

[14] Lavocat, "Introduzione," p. xiii.

[15] Cox, *Prodigious Muse*, pp. 18–19; Kolsky, "Moderata Fonte, Lucrezia Marinella, Giuseppe Passi," pp. 976–977 and p. 975, n. 11. On the relation of women to academies, see V. Cox, "Members, Muses, and Mascots: Women and the Italian Academies," in J. Everson, D. V. Reidy, and L. Sampson (eds.), *The Italian Academies, 1525–1700: Networks of Culture, Innovation, and Dissent* (Cambridge and Abingdon: MHRA and Routledge, 2016), pp. 132–167.

[16] Cox, *Women's Writing*, p. 207.

[17] See, for example, Benedetti, "Le *Essortationi* di Lucrezia Marinella," p. 382.

[18] Haskins, "A Portrait," p. 31.   [19] Lavocat, "Introduzione," p. xiv.

[20] Cox, *Prodigious Muse*, pp. 6, 11; Meredith K. Ray, *Daughters of Alchemy: Women and Scientific Culture in Early Modern Italy* (Cambridge, MA: Harvard University Press, 2015), pp. 93–110.

first and the last published, were hagiographies, biographies in prose or poetry of a number of saints and of the Virgin Mary that highlighted the inner lives and the spiritual authority of women; there was also a volume of religious verse (*Rime sacre* [*Sacred Rhymes*]) in 1603 that placed particular emphasis on women martyrs and their moral strength.[21] In addition to these devotional works, Marinella published fictional narratives in various genres: *L'Arcadia felice* (*Happy Arcadia*) (1605) is the first female-authored pastoral romance; *Amore innamorato, et impazzato, poema ... con gli argomenti, et allegorie a ciascun canto* (*Love in Love, and Impassioned*) (1618) is a mythological-allegorical epic poem; *L'Enrico, ovvero Bisanzio acquistato, poema eroico* (*Enrico, or Byzantium Conquered*) (1635) is a historical "heroic" poem. Finally, and most importantly for Marinella's standing as a philosopher, are two polemical treatises defending and encouraging the moral worth of women, written at the beginning and the end of her career: the *Nobiltà* and the *Essortationi alle donne et a gli altri, se a loro saranno a grado* (*Exhortations to Women and to Others if They Please*) (Venice: Francesco Valvasense, 1645). These reflect the interest in women apparent in the devotional and fictional works, especially an interest in women who possess political power, spiritual authority, and moral agency. The polemics both conceive of women as moral agents with rational motivations, spiritual aspirations, and political aims.[22]

What Marinella wrote, and how her works were received, were influenced by certain historical and political events and trends. The Council of Trent (1545–63), an ecumenical council of the Catholic Church that decided matters of doctrine and practice, issued a number of condemnations and decrees in response to criticisms from Protestantism. This, on most accounts, led to a turn toward religion and morality in Italian literature at the end of the sixteenth century. Because this turn included an emphasis on traditional gender roles, it is sometimes assumed that the norms of post-Tridentine literature were unfriendly to women. But one of the consequences of the moral rigor encouraged in the period was that it gave rise to a "congenial habitat for women," allowing them to write in a wide variety of genres from which they had effectively been excluded when the norms of those genres would have marked a woman as licentious.[23] This may explain in part why Marinella was able to publish so much, in such a diverse range of genres, and why the reception of her work was laudatory. She

---

[21] Cox, *Prodigious Muse*, pp. 71, 156–157.

[22] For an overview and discussion of Marinella's literary career, see Stephen Kolsky, "The Literary Career of Lucrezia Marinella (1571–1653): The Constraints of Gender and the Writing Woman," in F. W. Kent and C. Zika (eds.), *Rituals, Images and Words* (Turnhout: Brepols, 2013), pp. 325–342.

[23] Cox, *Prodigious Muse*, pp. 27–28, 134–136.

was able to use the norms of the post-Tridentine period to strategic advantage in the *Nobiltà*, criticizing men for their divergence from the moral ideals of the time.[24] There was, however, a backlash, with a rise in misogyny in response to the increasing participation of women in literary culture by the turn of the century that led to an increase in their polemical writing.[25] That was the context in which Marinella wrote the *Nobiltà* in 1600–1. As the seventeenth century progressed, the climate for women as authors deteriorated, as it became more difficult to find powerful women as patrons, and publishers became less willing to print feminist work without such patronage.[26] This may explain why Marinella's second polemic, the *Essortationi* (1645), was couched in terms that suggested that women should accept their traditional roles in the household and as help-meets to men, although, as I will argue in Sections 7 and 8, the message of the *Essortationi* is also feminist.

Marinella's reputation was founded on brilliance, learning, and religious devotion. As a woman of literary and philosophical accomplishment Marinella was not unique, but she was exceptional. Her work was held in unusually high esteem by her contemporaries. As early as 1596 her intellect was praised in print by Girolamo Mercurio in his *La commare o riccoglitrice* (*La commare, or, the Midwife*).[27] Pietro Paolo Ribera lauded Marinella in 1609 as one of a series of "heroic" women, and emphasized her "noble and most religious ways."[28] In 1620 Francesco Agostino Della Chiesa characterized Marinella as the "sole phoenix of our time," remarking on her unequaled eloquence and erudition in his compendium of biographies of women writers, *Theatro delle donne letterate* (*Theatre of Learned Women*). Cristofano Bronzino praised Marinella as a "glory of our century, with that excellent discourse, entitled *The Nobility and Virtue of Women*," adding that she was "highly versed in natural and moral philosophy, devout, humble"; he took her *Nobiltà* as a model for his dialogue, *Della dignità e nobiltà delle donne* (*On the Dignity and Nobility of Women*).[29]

Despite this extensive and effusive praise, Marinella did not altogether escape the hostility that confronted many women writers, nor the disappointments of

---

[24] A. Dialeti, "A Woman Defending Women: Breaking with Tradition in Lucrezia Marinella's *La nobiltà, et eccellenze delle donne*," in A. Cagnolati (ed.), *A Portrait of a Renaissance Feminist: Lucrezia Marinella's Life and Works* (Rome: Aracne, 2013), pp. 69, 97.

[25] Cox, *Prodigious Muse*, p. 49.　　[26] Cox, *Women's Writing*, pp. 207, 222.

[27] Haskins, "A Portrait," p. 24 and n. 57.

[28] Cox, *Women's Writing*, pp. 141–143; Haskins, "A Portrait," p. 24.

[29] C. Bronzino, *Della dignità e nobiltà delle donne* (*On the Dignity and Nobility of Women*): (Florence: Zanobi Pignoni, 1622), first week, first day, p. 30, cited in Lavocat, "Introduzione," p. xv. See also Haskins, "A Portrait," p. 24. On the *Nobiltà* as a model for Bronzino, see R. Gogol, "The Literary Exchange between Lucrezia Marinella and Cristofano Bronzini," in L. Marinella, *De' gesti eroici e della vita meravigliosa della Serafica S. Caterina da Siena*, A. Maggi (ed.) (Ravenna: Longo, 2011), p. 218.

every writer. Some contested the authorship of her *Vita di Maria Vergine* (1602); the rumors were widespread enough that in a foreword to Marinella's *Arcadia felice* (1605) the publisher defended Marinella against "malicious slanderers."[30] Marinella may have had this episode in mind in the *Essortationi* when she deplores the inclination of men to doubt the authorship of learned women.[31] Even among feminists, Marinella was not immune to criticism: Anna Maria van Schurman, in a letter to Andrea Rivetus in 1638, referred to Marinella's *Nobiltà* as "extraordinary" (*insignem*), but also disapproved, saying that it was incompatible with virginal modesty, which perhaps says more about van Schurman than it does about the *Nobiltà*.[32]

Although Marinella's fame diminished soon after her death, in the late seventeenth and early eighteenth centuries some of her verse was reissued in anthologies of women poets.[33] Marinella appears in Bayle's *Dictionary* as "a Venetian lady who had considerable intelligence, and published among other books a work entitled *The Nobility* .... she carried the convictions of her sex, not merely to equality, as other authors did, but also to superiority."[34] By the nineteenth century her reputation was largely eclipsed, along with the reputations of many women philosophers.

In this Element the focus is on Marinella's most philosophical and feminist works: the *Nobiltà* and the *Essortationi*. I read both polemics as arguments for the worth and the abilities of women. The *Essortationi* appears to be much more conservative and includes specific denials of some of the claims of the *Nobiltà*. This leads some to construe it as a rejection of the vehemently pro-woman stance of the *Nobiltà*.[35] I agree, however, with those scholars who see clear evidence in the *Essortationi* that, as Amy Sinclair writes, it is "an extension of the [*Nobiltà*'s] targeted and explicit critique of the mechanisms used by male writers to propagate and reinforce the notion of women's subservience and their appropriate confinement within the home."[36] The apparent retractions are, on this interpretation, likely to be concessions to the changing context of

---

[30] Cox, *Women's Writing*, pp. 207, 219, 368, n. 224.   [31] Marinella, *Exhortations*, p. 57.

[32] L. Panizza, "Introduction," in A. Dunhill (ed. and trans.), *Lucrezia Marinella: The Nobility and Excellence of Women and the Defects and Vices of Men* (Chicago: University of Chicago Press, 1999), p. 31 and n. 67.

[33] Lavocat, "Introduzione," pp. xiv–xv, n. 90; Panizza, "Introduction," pp. 31–33.

[34] P. Bayle, *Dictionnaire historique et critique*, 3rd ed. (Rotterdam: Michel Bohm, 1720), vol. III, pp. 1937–1938, translation mine. Cited in Lavocat, "Introduzione," p. xiv, n. 43.

[35] See Benedetti, "Introduction" in Marinella, *Exhortations*, for the view that we should not "take Marinella's texts at face value when they proclaim principles appealing to twenty-first-century readers but ... dismiss or creatively deconstruct them if they let us down" (p. 34). Benedetti treats the *Essortationi* as a "recantation" of the views Marinella expressed in the *Nobiltà*.

[36] A. Sinclair, "Latin in Lucrezia Marinella's *Essortationi alle donne* (1645): Subverting the Voice of Authority," in E. Del Soldato and A. Rizzi (eds.), *City, Court, Academy: Language Choice in Early Modern Italy* (London: Routledge, 2017), p. 117. For a similar view, see P. Malpezzi Price

publication for women in the seventeenth century, concessions that are always followed by an undermining of their surface message, as we will see in Sections 7 and 8.[37]

3 Context

3.1 The *querelle des femmes*

Marinella's *Nobiltà* and her *Essortationi* were contributions to the *querelle des femmes*, a debate about the nature and the worth of women that unfolded in different phases in Europe from the medieval through the early modern period. Contributions to the *querelle* appeared in Latin and a number of vernacular languages, both in printed editions and as manuscripts that circulated in courts. Both men and women participated in the debate in a variety of genres; women almost always defended their sex, while men, both clerics and secular authors, wrote misogynist as well as pro-woman works.[38] Pro-woman contributions to the *querelle* introduce the claims and the arguments that are the origins of feminist theory in Europe.

The *querelle* began, on most accounts, with Christine de Pizan's response to *Le roman de la rose* (*The Romance of the Rose*), an allegorical poem by Guillaume de Lorris and Jean de Meung, written in the thirteenth century, that characterized women as unfaithful, deceptive, vain, loquacious, and lubricious.[39] De Pizan was critical of the *Roman*, objecting to the poem's obscene language, unfounded generalizations about women, and its incoherent suggestion that men should both pursue women and avoid them as "venemous serpent[s]."[40] That incoherence was characteristic of many works that represented women both as ideals and as distractions or temptations to men, with courtly love (a medieval code of attitudes to love and of behaviors appropriate for the nobility) and gallantry as one expression of masculinity, and misogyny as another. The exchange between the advocates for the *Roman* and de Pizan effectively established a structure for the *querelle*, in which those arguing for the worth of women were responding to those

---

and C. Ristaino, *Lucrezia Marinella and the "Querelle des Femmes" in Seventeenth-Century Italy* (Madison, NJ: Fairleigh Dickinson University Press, 2008), pp. 154–155.

[37] On the conservatism of the *Exhortations* and the likelihood that it was a response to political circumstances, see L. Benedetti, "Arcangela Tarabotti e Lucrezia Marinella: appunti per un dialogo mancato," *Modern Language Notes*, 129:3S (2014), S95.

[38] J. Kelly, "Early Feminist Theory and the 'Querelle des femmes,' 1400–1789," *Signs*, 8:1 (1982), pp. 4–28. See also J. J. Parry, "Introduction," in A. Cappellanus, *The Art of Courtly Love* (New York: Columbia University Press, 1960), and C. McWebb, *Debating the "Roman de la rose": A Critical Anthology* (New York: Routledge, 2007).

[39] D. F. Hult, "The *Roman de la rose*, Christine de Pizan, and the *querelle des femmes*," in C. Dinshaw and D. Wallace (eds.), *The Cambridge Companion to Medieval Women's Writing* (Cambridge: Cambridge University Press, 2003), p. 2.

[40] Hult, "The *Roman*," p. 2; see also C. de Pizan, *Debate of the "Romance of the Rose,"* D. F. Hult (ed. and trans.) (Chicago: University of Chicago Press, 2010).

asserting the worthlessness of women, and as a result pro-woman works often adopted the terms of the misogynists and were structured as replies to their claims and arguments.

Both Marinella's *Nobiltà* and her *Essortationi* are contributions to this debate. In the sixteenth century, preceding Marinella's *Nobiltà*, a diverse and extensive range of feminist literature was produced in Italy – or, written elsewhere, circulated widely in Italy – as part of the *querelle*.[41] These were popular works, aimed at an educated audience outside the universities. Feminist works were often dedicated to a woman with some political power or influence, and it is likely that in some cases women commissioned the work, an indication perhaps of the views they held but could not publicly express.[42] Such works emerged both in the republics of early modern Italy (e.g., Venice) and in the courts (especially of Ferrara and Mantova). The aims of these works were diverse: to demonstrate the rhetorical capacity of the author, to entertain, to please a patron and hence to gain some advancement, or to convince an audience of a conclusion. Two of the most popular and influential were a polemical treatise by Henricus Cornelius Agrippa, *De Nobilitate & Praecellentia Foeminei Sexus* (*On the Nobility and Preeminence of the Female Sex*), published in Antwerp in 1529 and translated into Italian by 1545, and a dialogue by Baldassare Castiglione, *Libro del cortegiano* (*The Courtier*), published in Venice in 1528, in which the third book represents a debate about women, including the perspective of a man arguing for the equality of women.[43] Their influence on Marinella is evident, as we will see.

---

[41] For a discussion of the genre of defenses of women, see F. Daenens, "Superiore perché inferiore: il paradosso della superiorità della donna in alcuni trattati italiani del Cinquecento," in V. Gentili (ed.), *Trasgressione Tragica e Norma Domestica* (Rome: Edizioni di Storia Letteratura, 1983), pp. 11–124.

[42] For examples of women with political power and their relations with pro-woman authors, see J. Manca, "'Constantia et Forteza': Eleanora d'Aragona's Famous Matrons," *Notes in the History of Art*, 19:2 (2000), pp. 13–20; V. Cox, "Gender and Eloquence in Ercole de' Roberti's *Portia and Brutus*," *Renaissance Quarterly*, 62 (2009), pp. 66–67, 88–90; S. Kolsky, *The Ghost of Boccaccio: Writings on Famous Women in Renaissance Italy* (Turnhout: Brepols Publishers, 2005), pp. 148–170; L. Chiappini, *Eleanora d'Aragona, prima Duchessa di Ferrara* (Rovigo: S.T.E.R., 1956). Carolyn James points out that a woman with political power had to be more careful than a noble woman of intellectual interests but without political power (e.g., Margherita Cantelmo) in appearing to embrace radical ideas; C. James, "Margherita Cantelmo and the Worth of Women in Renaissance Italy," in K. Green and C. Mews (eds.), *Virtue Ethics for Women 1250–1500* (Dordrecht: Springer Netherlands, 2011), pp. 145–163, 147.

[43] Agrippa, *Della nobiltà e eccellenza delle donne, dalla lingua francese nella italiana tradotto con una Oratione di M. Allessandro Piccolomini in lode delle medesime* (trans. Coccio) (Venice: appresso Gabriel Giolito de Ferrari, 1545); Castiglione, *Il Cortegiano di Baldassare Castiglione*, A. Busi and C. Covito (trans. and eds.) (Milano: Rizzoli, 1993).

3.2 Marinella's Sources

In the *Nobiltà* Marinella makes reference to an astonishing number of sources – literary, theological, and philosophical – to support her claims. Of Italians she mentions not only Dante, Petrarch, and Boccaccio but also closer contemporaries: Sperone Speroni, Ercole Tasso, and Torquato Tasso, among many. She draws on medieval philosophers, theologians, and mystics: Saint Bernard, Hildegard of Bingen, Saint Bridget, Saint Catherine of Siena (the subject of a hagiography by Marinella), and Peter Lombard. Of ancient authors she cites Epictetus, Cicero, Plutarch, Speusippus, Ovid, Porphyry, Livy, Diogenes Laertius, Seneca, and many others; but most often when she wishes to invoke philosophical authority for a position, she turns to Plato (or Socrates) and, especially, to Aristotle. Marinella's sources for Platonism (most evident in her arguments about beauty – see Section 7) were the translations and commentaries by Ficino and the work of Leone Ebreo (Yehudah Abarbanel or Abravanel), in particular his *Dialoghi d'amore* (*Dialogues on Love*) (Rome, 1535). The works of Aristotle she read in Latin translations (e.g., *Politics* translated by Leonardo Bruni, *Nicomachean Ethics* translated by Ioanne Bernardo Feliciano, and the biological works translated by Teodoro Gaza).[44]

Marinella's reliance on Aristotle in the *Nobiltà*, the *Essortationi*, and the literary works is especially striking because she is so critical of him in the *Nobiltà* for his views on the physiology of women. She often and unapologetically relies on his authority to make her arguments for the worth of women. The *Nobiltà* begins with a reference to Book VIII of Aristotle's *Metaphysics*, and draws on his *Ethics*, his *Politics*, and his biological works to defend women against their critics, including Aristotle himself.[45] In the note to the readers that prefaces *l'Enrico* she says, "I aimed to fashion my poem according to Aristotle's directions in his *Poetics*."[46] The eighth *Essortationi* is effectively an application of Book VIII of Aristotle's *Politics* to the social circumstances of seventeenth-century Venice.[47]

---

[44] Benedetti, in the Introduction to the *Exhortations* (p. 27), points out that Marinella used the translation of Aristotle's *Politics* by Leonardo Bruni; it includes the commentary of St. Thomas Aquinas (L. Bruni, *Politicorum libri VIII latine ex versione Leonardi Aretini* [Roma: E. Silber, 1492]). Marinella used the translation of Aristotle's *Nicomachean Ethics* by Giovanni Bernardo Feliciano, first published in 1543 (Venice: Aldine, 1543) and reprinted many times.

[45] L. Marinella, *The Nobility and Excellence of Women, and the Defects and Vices of Men* (Chicago: University of Chicago Press, 1999), p. 45.

[46] L. Marinella, *Enrico; or, Byzantium Conquered: A Heroic Poem*, M. Galli Stampino (ed. and trans.), (Chicago: University of Chicago Press, 2009), p. 77.

[47] Rebecca Langlands, in an unpublished paper from 1995, "Lucrezia Marinella's Feminism and the Authority of the Classics," first explored Marinella's reliance on Aristotle. Annika Willer suggests that the second (1601) edition of the *Nobiltà* reduced religious arguments and emphasized the discussion of Plato and Aristotle (A. Willer, "Silent Deletions: The Two Different

It is important also to acknowledge certain misogynist works as sources, and stimulants, for Marinella's *Nobiltà* in particular. A seminal misogynist text was Boccaccio's *Il Corbaccio* (*The Corbaccio*), which remained extremely influential in the sixteenth century. In 1586 "Onofrio Filarco" published in Padua a treatise titled *Vera narratione delle operationi delle donne* (*A True Account of the Operations of Women*), "slandering women quite explicitly"; soon after in Treviso Cipriano Giambelli argued for the superiority of men in his *Discorso intorno alla maggioranza dell'huomo e della donna* (*Discourse on the Superiority of Men, and of Women*) (1589). The most important misogynist source for Marinella was, however, a vicious and lengthy treatise that was "an admonitory diatribe against women's vices, *I donneschi difetti* (*Womanly Defects*) by the academician and *letterato* Giuseppe Passi."[48] This was the work in response to which Marinella wrote the *Nobiltà*.

3.3 Marinella's Interlocutors

When Marinella set out to write the *Nobiltà* she was doing so not only in response to misogynist publications, but also with the resources of an existing tradition in defense of women. At the end of the fifteenth and the beginning of the sixteenth centuries in northern Italy, a number of manuscripts in Latin or the vernacular dedicated to women of power and arguing for the worth of women circulated: Goggio's *De laudibus mulierum* (*In Praise of Women*) (ca.1487), Strozzi's *Defensione delle donne contro i maledici loro calunniatori: in due libri* (*A Defense of Women from their Cursed Slanderers*) (ca.1501), Equicola's *De mulieribus* (*On Women*) (ca.1501). There is some indication that these works were presented in courts and that they gave rise to discussions there and in the academies and literary salons, so that by the middle of the sixteenth century the question of the worth of women was a matter of public debate.[49] Two shifts in particular made women's access to intellectual life in the sixteenth century possible: the transfer of learning outside of universities, from which women were excluded, to "princely courts, where women were present as powerful patrons" and the erosion of "traditional prohibitions against the marriage of scholars" and the transmission of this scholarly knowledge from humanist fathers to daughters.[50] Aside from the works of Agrippa and Castiglione mentioned in Section 3.1, defenses of women were published by Vincenzo Maggi, Galeazzo Flavio Capra, Lodovico Domenichi, Domenico Bruni da Pistoia, Francesco Caruso, and many others, establishing a genre of literature that was "quintessentially courtly" and associated with

Editions of Lucrezia Marinella's *La Nobiltà et l'eccellenza delle donne*," *Bruniana & Campanelliana*, 19:1 [2013], pp. 207–219, 215–216).

[48] Cox, *Women's Writing*, p. 173.   [49] Dialeti, "A Woman Defending Women," pp. 70–71.

[50] G. Pomata, "Was There a Querelle des femmes in Early Modern Medicine?" *Arenal: Revista de Historia de las Mujeres*, 20:3 (2013), pp. 219–220.

attitudes of gallantry toward women; particularly in the courts, this gallantry and an "appreciation of women's capacity for 'heroic' or 'virile' attainment" were taken as marks of civility.[51] Defenses of women may be seen as an outgrowth of courtly literature, in which encomia of individual women, imagined or represented as ideals of beauty and virtue, were extended to exalt the entire sex.[52] The genre promoted a Counter-Reformation moral ideal involving piety and self-restraint that had a "new relevance for men"; that is, virtuous women became models not only for other women but also for men.[53] Boccaccio's *De claris mulieribus* (*On Famous Women*) listed examples of women, historical and fictional, whose virtues and accomplishments were taken to demonstrate the worth of their sex. It is worth remarking that Boccaccio was not unique in publishing both a misogynist work and a work lauding the virtues of women (for example, Passi also did); the two attitudes of gallantry and superiority were not far distant. The debate about women was a "privileged field of meaning for the self-fashioning of male *letterati*" whether they took a pro-feminist position as a demonstration of gallantry, or an anti-feminist position as a demonstration of dominance.[54]

3.4 Methods

The methods of feminist works in the sixteenth century encompassed three standard strategies: (1) listing examples (*exempla*), often drawn from Boccaccio's *De claris mulieribus*, of courageous, modest, inventive, or loyal women, and women who had exercised political power effectively and justly, to demonstrate the possibility that women might possess intellectual and moral virtues and have the capacities for political rule, (2) invoking authorities, secular and scriptural, philosophical, theological and literary, to demonstrate that authority is on the side of the equality or superiority of women, and (3) reasoning, namely arguments intended to convince the reader of the truth of these claims. While the authors do not often name a fourth method, they do regularly employ it: (4) the raising of doubts about received opinion. Marinella uses each of these methods, not only as techniques to persuade her audience of her conclusions, but also as means to demonstrate her own intellectual authority.

---

[51] Cox, *Women's Writing*, pp. 92, 168.

[52] A. Cagnolati, "Un duello in punta di penna: strategie antimisogine nella *Nobiltà*" in A. Cagnolati (ed.), *A Portrait of a Renaissance Feminist* (Rome: Aracne, 2013), p. 47; G. Zonta, *Trattati del Cinquecento sulla donna* (Bari: Laterza 1913), p. 375; A. Chemello, "La donna, il modello, l'immaginario: Moderata Fonte e Lucezia Marinella" in *Nel cerchio della luna: Figure di donna in alcuni testi del XVI secolo*, M. Zancan (ed.) (Venice: Marsilio, 1983), p.153.

[53] Cox, *Prodigious Muse*, p. 30.   [54] Cox, *Women's Writing*, p. 177.

In Marinella's *Nobiltà* we can see the skill she had acquired through her hagiographic writing in acclaiming the virtues, applied not to an individual, but to an entire sex. At the same time, we can see the influence of the literary genre of the invective perfected by Petrarch (of which Boccaccio's *Il Corbaccio* is an example) in her sustained and diverse criticisms of men. In the *Nobiltà* and the *Essortationi* she writes with her audience in mind: on the one hand, she directs herself often to women, and in writing in the vernacular clearly anticipated that she would be read by women; on the other hand, she quotes Latin authors in Latin, and Greek authors in Latin translation, which suggests strongly that she expected men, as well as women, to take an interest in her arguments.

4 Nobility and Superiority

4.1 Framing the Question

When authors engaged in the *querelle* considered the question of the worth of women, several competing answers were available to them: (i) the sexes are equal in all respects, (ii) one sex is superior to the other, (iii) the sexes are equal in at least one respect, but one is superior in some respects, or (iv) some subset of one sex is superior to most of the members of the other. Marinella develops a version of the second response, arguing that women are superior to men. While some commentators suppose that this was an unusual stance for those on the pro-woman side of the debate, there were a number of authors who made arguments for the superiority of women in some respect, even while asserting the fundamental equality of men and women in a shared capacity for reason distinctive of human beings.[55] The apparent tension between saying that women were essentially equal to men, and that they were nonetheless superior to men in some respects, is lessened when we distinguish between metaphysical claims of equality (i.e., that, in principle, the two sexes have the same capacities) and practical claims of equality (i.e., that each sex can realize those capacities equally well). That is, an author might allow that the capacity for reason in men and women was the same, but argue that women's bodies or circumstances allowed them to better exercise reason. But Marinella makes only the smallest concession to that view, by acknowledging that the sexes have a shared capacity for reason, while arguing that the souls of women are nobler.

Some have suggested that claims of superiority of the sort made by Marinella can be reduced to equality claims because they are rhetorical overstatements of

---

[55] For the claim that it was unusual, see M. Angenot, *Les Champions des femmes: examen du discours sur la supériorité des femmes, 1400–1800* (Montréal: Presses de l'Université du Québec, 1977) and C. Jordan, *Renaissance Feminism: Literary Texts and Political Models* (Ithaca, NY: Cornell University Press, 1990).

the worth of women.[56] In other words, some arguments for the superiority of women might not have been intended to persuade their audience that women were superior to men, but rather that they were equal. On the one hand, Marinella casts her arguments in such a way as to suggest that she intends us to take her claims seriously, and literally. On the other, the polemical nature of the *Nobiltà* and its imitation of the structure of misogynist texts and arguments (especially those of Passi) may indicate that she was aiming to undermine claims of male superiority as much as to establish the superiority of women.[57]

4.2 Superiority and Nobility

For Marinella, the question of the superiority of women centres on the notion of *nobiltà*, which is usually translated as "nobility." I follow that practice, but "nobility" has to be understood as a technical term for Marinella. The title of her polemic, *La nobiltà et l'eccellenza delle donne, co' diffetti et mancamenti de gli huomini*, resembles the titles of a number of earlier and later defenses of women in which references to the nobility, dignity, virtue, or worth of women figure largely.[58] Nobility and excellence, or virtue, are correlate terms; this becomes clear when we consider Dante's discussion of *nobilitade* in *Convivio* IV, which is likely to be the source of the notion in the Renaissance. Nobility, on Dante's account, is a capacity or potentiality to develop the human virtues, and excellences are those virtues. So Marinella, in attributing nobility to women, was asserting that they have an intrinsic worth and elevated moral status. And, in insisting that women are nobler than men, she was suggesting that while men do in fact have this human capacity for virtue, the capacity of women is greater. Moreover, when she rejected the suggestion by Tasso and others that only women who were patrician, or of the highest social status, were "noble" in this sense, she was aligning herself with Dante in treating nobility not as a social

---

[56] For example, see I. Ducharme, "Marguerite Buffet: lectrice de la Querelle des femmes," in I. Brouard-Arends (ed.), *Lectrices d'ancien régime* (Rennes: Presses Universitaires de Rennes, 2003), p. 333.

[57] On arguments for superiority prior to Marinella, see S. Kolsky, *The Ghost of Boccaccio: Writings on Famous Women in Renaissance Italy* (Turnhout: Brepols, 2005), p. 171–172.

[58] This is the title of the 1601 edition; the first edition, in 1600, has the slightly different title: *Le* [sic] *nobiltà et eccellenze delle donne, et i diffetti, e mancamenti de gli huomini*. Examples of other pro-woman works include: Galeazzo Flavio Capella [Capra], *Della eccellenza et dignità delle donne*, M. L. Doglio (ed.) (Rome: Bulzoni Editore, [1525] 2001); H. C. Agrippa, *De nobilitate & praecellentia foeminei sexus* (Antwerp, 1529); Vincenzo Maggi, *Un brieve trattato dell'eccellentia delle donne* (Brescia: Damiano de Turlini, 1545); Lodovico Domenichi, *La nobiltà delle donne* (Venice: Giolito, 1549/1551); Torquato Tasso, *Discorso della virtù feminile e donnesca*, M. L. Doglio (ed.) (Palermo: Sellerio Editore, [1582] 1997); and Bronzino, *Della dignità e nobiltà delle donne*.

status but rather as a natural human capacity, although a capacity that might differ in degree between individuals.[59]

The project of Dante's *Convivio* IV was to demonstrate that nobility was not a function of wealth or an inherited status, but rather a moral and intellectual capacity present in some measure in all human beings. He says "human nobility is none other than the 'seed of happiness' [placed by God] in the ready soul, that is, the soul whose body is perfectly disposed throughout," and makes clear that he is working in an Aristotelian framework by pointing out that this definition includes all four causes (material, formal, efficient, and final).[60] The formal cause or essence of nobility is to be the seed or source or origin of happiness; its efficient cause is God, who bestows this seed on the human soul; the material cause is the "ready soul," which is the human soul in a body that is perfectly (i.e., completely) disposed to receive it; and the final cause is happiness – the actuality of which the seed or capacity is the potentiality.[61]

Nobility is then a capacity for certain human dispositions and activities, both moral and intellectual – these are the virtues, which are the "fruits" of the "seed" that is nobility. The relation of nobility to virtue is thus that of potentiality to actuality. But nobility is not always manifested in virtue, because while it is necessary for the development of virtue, it is not sufficient. Human virtues emerge only under certain conditions. The first of these is a "ready soul," which is a human soul in a body that is perfectly formed in the sense that it has all the organs necessary for human activities, and a complexion, or physiological character, optimally adapted for the activities of the soul. When Dante says that "there is nobility wherever there is virtue, and not virtue wherever there is nobility,"[62] he means that the virtues are acquired only when the capacity that is nobility is correctly cultivated and habituated in a soul that inhabits a complete and well-functioning body; nobility does not inevitably or necessarily yield the virtues. So while every person will have nobility in some degree in virtue of being a person, every person will not actualize that capacity to acquire the virtues to the same degree.

If nobility belongs to every human soul, but individuals vary with respect to the virtues they manifest, we might ask what is responsible for those variations. One determining factor is the degree of "purity" of the soul, which is a function, in part, of the complexion of the body, namely, the relative proportion of the

---

[59] See Tasso, *Discorso*, p. 63.
[60] Dante (Alighieri, Dante), *Convivio: A Dual-Language Critical Edition*, A. Frisardi (ed. and trans.) (Cambridge: Cambridge University Press, 2018), Book IV: xx, 9–10.
[61] See Aristotle, *Physics* II. 3 195a15-26 for the distinction among four kinds of cause.
[62] Dante, *Convivio* IV: xix, 5.

different elements that enter into the constitution of the body.[63] Nobility, on Dante's account, is both a natural power or capacity and a gift of God.[64] It is the natural process of human generation – conception and embryogenesis – that produces a body that is "perfectly disposed" to receive a human soul. The soul, however, is produced in the body by God (and not simply by means of embryological development). As soon as the soul enters the body it receives the passive intellect, which is the human capacity to understand the essences of things.[65] A pure soul is one in which the passive intellect that is received from God is "detached from and free of all corporeal shadow," with the result that "divine goodness increases within it." Dante identifies the capacity to receive the passive intellect, together with the intellect itself, as the "seed of happiness," which, as we have seen, is itself nobility.[66]

When Marinella claims, then, that women are "nobler" than men and more "excellent" she is writing in a tradition where human nobility is understood to be in the first instance a rational capacity, with implications for moral excellence because reason is a requisite for virtue. The human body must be complete and well constituted to receive nobility, and to serve as the instrument of the soul. While, then, nobility is a feature of the soul, it is a feature that is influenced by the character of the body; we will see in Section 6 how Marinella elaborates on this point to argue for the superiority of women. And nobility as a capacity is best recognized when it is actualized in the virtues; in Section 8 we will consider how Marinella develops her claim that women are superior with respect to both the intellectual and the moral virtues.

4.3 The Origins of Superiority

Because nobility is a feature of the human soul and the foundation of women's superiority on Marinella's account, the origins of that superiority lie with the efficient cause of the soul. Marinella, Like Dante, believed that God was that efficient cause. She assumes that there is a hierarchy of created beings, which differ in "degrees of perfection": "Angels are extremely noble, man less noble, the heavens noble, the earth extremely ignoble."[67] Within the class of animals, Marinella says, "some are more and some less perfect."[68] All of these variations in perfection or nobility are possible because "[i]t is the creator who decides which things are of less value and which are worthier, and more particularly, which have a less noble Idea and which a more remarkable one."[69] Although,

---

[63] Dante, *Convivio* IV: xxi, 7.   [64] Dante, *Convivio* IV: xxi, 1.
[65] Dante, *Convivio* IV: xxi, 4–5.   [66] Dante, *Convivio* IV: xxii, 4.
[67] L. Marinella, *The Nobility and Excellence of Women, and the Defects and Vices of Men*, A. Dunhill (trans.) (Chicago: The University of Chicago Press, 1999), p. 52.
[68] Marinella, *Nobility*, p. 53.   [69] Marinella, *Nobility*, p. 52; trans. modified.

then, God is the efficient cause of every created being, he "had different Ideas for them when He produced them"; the result is that the essence or soul of different beings will have different values.[70]

Marinella also drew on a tradition that mixed Aristotelian, Platonist, and other ancient elements, in which the soul is first an Idea in the mind of God, which may be more or less noble.[71] Marinella explains that the Ideas "are the external exemplars and images of things, whose proper place lies in the mind of the supreme power before their creation."[72] These Ideas, or Forms, are the models on which individual instances of a kind are formed. They serve two philosophical purposes: one metaphysical, insofar as it is participation in a Form that makes an individual the kind of thing it is; and the second epistemological, in that it is recognizing that an individual participates in the Form that allows us to know it as an instance of the kind. So, for example, there is an Idea or Form of the snowy owl, which includes all and only those features necessary to and distinctive of the snowy owl. Any individual snowy owl will be a member of the kind in virtue of "participating" in that Form – namely, possessing those features. And one will be able to recognize that an individual bird is a snowy owl only through some acquaintance with the Form.

The notion that these Forms, or Ideas, reside "in the mind of the supreme power before their creation" is a later formulation, as is the suggestion Marinella makes that these Ideas are the forms of *individuals*, rather than the essences of species (which would be identical in every individual of the species). She is drawing on Leone Ebreo (Yehudah Abravanel) who, she says, "refers to Ideas as divine precognition of things produced, because before God creates things He has an image in his mind of what He wants to create."[73] To explain how these Ideas are transmitted to the individual in creation Marinella draws an analogy between creation as performed by God and creation as performed by an artist or an architect, who will also have a "thing or image" which is "an idea or pattern" in their mind prior to the creation of a painting or a palace. Her language in describing these Ideas is strongly visual and aligns what is morally good with what is perceptibly beautiful; the terms she employs to refer to the relative value of these ideas in the minds of human makers refer to the aesthetic as well as the moral worth of the artifacts produced – a palace that is "superb, well-proportioned" will be nobler than one that is "poor, disproportionate" and a painting of a "lovely nymph" will be nobler than the dwelling of "a rustic and deformed satyr."[74] This conflation of aesthetic and moral value

---

[70] Marinella, *Nobility*, p. 52.
[71] For a discussion of this tradition, see A. N. M. Rich, "The Platonic Ideas as the Thoughts of God," *Mnemosyne*, Fourth Series 7:2 (1954), pp. 123–133.
[72] Marinella, *Nobility*, p. 53. [73] Marinella, *Nobility*, p. 53. [74] Marinella, *Nobility*, p. 53.

resonates, as we will see in Section 7, with Marinella's emphasis on the beauty of women as evidence of the nobility of their souls.

The fundamental superiority claim that Marinella makes about women is thus that their souls are nobler than men's, because the Idea in the mind of God of a woman is a nobler Idea than that of a man. Since the Idea when transmitted to the individual is their soul, the soul of a woman is nobler than a man's. Two implications of this claim are worth bearing in mind as we continue. First, Marinella seems to be working both with a Platonic conception of the soul as the form, in the sense of a manifestation of an Idea in a corporeal body, and with an Aristotelian conception of the soul as form or essence, in the sense of the actuality of a living body (since she refers to the soul as the "nature and substance" of a person). This will be important when we consider the beauty argument in Section 7. Second, Marinella is exceptional among pro-woman authors in arguing for the superior nobility of the souls of women, since most assume that because men and women possess the same rational capacity, which is the peculiarly human faculty of the soul, their souls are the same. In the next section we will consider her views on the soul and ask how she reconciles the claim that the rational faculty of the soul of men and women is the same with her assertion that the souls of women are nobler.

5 Soul

5.1 The Identity of the Rational Faculty

We have seen in Section 4.2 that Dante identified the capacity of the human soul to receive the intellect from God, and that intellect itself, with nobility. This identification of human nobility with the human intellect explains in part the first and most fundamental argument employed by most pro-woman authors in the *querelle des femmes*: the argument from the common possession of the rational faculty of soul. Two influential statements of the equality of the sexes that predate Marinella make clear the significance of reason as a capacity. The first, in which the intellect is represented as a gift of God, is found in Agrippa's treatise *De nobilitate*:

> [God] has attributed to both man and woman an identical soul, which sexual difference does not at all affect. Woman has been allotted the same intelligence, reason, and power of speech as man . . . .[75]

The second is in Castiglione's dialogue *Il Cortegiano*, where the point is expressed in natural rather than divine terms:

---

[75] H. C. Agrippa, *Declamation on the Nobility and Preeminence of the Female Sex*, A. Rabil, Jr. (ed. and trans.) (Chicago: University of Chicago Press, 1996 [1529]), p. 43.

For just as no stone can be more perfectly a stone than another, as regards the essence stone, nor one piece of wood more perfectly wood than another piece – so one man cannot be more perfectly man than another; and consequently the male will not be more perfect than the female as regards their formal substance, because the one and the other are included under the species man, and that in which one differs from another is an accident and is not of the essence.[76]

Where Agrippa specifies "the same intelligence, reason, and power of speech" as the content of the "identical soul" that is shared by men and women, he is making clear that these are the powers peculiar to the human (as opposed to the animal or vegetable) soul. In sharing these powers, which he claims are undifferentiated by sex, women share in the same human essence as men. Castiglione is making the same point: that the "formal substance," or essence, of human beings (the rational faculty or intellect) is identical whether a person is male or female. Moreover, Marinella's near-contemporary, Moderata Fonte, is quoted by Marinella as asserting the same point in her work, *Floridoro*, with the addition that if the formal substance is the same we should expect the capabilities of women to equal those of men.

Many pro-woman authors argue for the superiority of women in some respect only after maintaining the equality of the sexes with respect to the rational soul. This was because a shared essence – the rational soul – established men and women as the same in kind, possessing the same species essence. In the context of misogynist literature that ventured close to claiming women were more like animals than persons, this commitment to a shared human essence was significant. Marinella acknowledged this tradition, saying "if we speak as philosophers we will say that man's soul is equally noble to women's because both are of the same species and therefore of the same nature and substance."[77] She did not dispute that the rational souls of men and women are identical in kind; she makes that clear by saying that "women have the same rational souls as men."[78] She does, however, dispute the inference that there is no difference in the souls of the sexes: "I do not agree with this opinion ... I would say that women's souls were created nobler than men's, as can be seen from the effect they have and from the beauty of their bodies."[79] We will consider her contention that the evidence of the greater nobility of women's souls is to be found in the "effects" of their souls (Section 8) and in the beauty of their bodies (Section 7). In this section the focus is on just what Marinella means by this assertion of superiority rather equality of the soul.

---

[76] B. Castiglione, *The Book of the Courtier*, C. S. Singleton (trans.) (New York: Doubleday, 1959), p. 214.

[77] Marinella, *Nobility*, p. 55.   [78] Marinella, *Nobility*, p. 37.   [79] Marinella, *Nobility*, p. 55.

She addresses the concern that allowing for differences in the nobility of the sexes might seem to imply that they were different species (or subspecies). Her reply is that it is possible that some souls within a species might be nobler than others from birth (citing Peter Lombard [*Sentences* 2.32]). God, as the efficient cause of human beings, is able to bestow on some individuals within the human species a soul that is intrinsically superior to the souls of other individuals: "Among the many kinds of animals and living things, for example, some are more and some less perfect. All, however, depend on the same cause [i.e. God]. If this is the case, as in truth it is, why should not woman be nobler than man and have a rarer and more excellent Idea than he?"[80] To have a "more excellent Idea" is to have a better soul, since the soul is the Idea or form of the body. The point is that it does not follow from the fact that God is the efficient cause of both sexes that the sexes must be equally noble, since God is the cause of all living things and yet there is a difference in the nobility of the different species he produces.

This response does not seem to address the objection that while different animal species may have different degrees of nobility precisely because they are different in species, since men and women are members of the same species they should not differ in nobility, assuming that nobility is a feature of the species form or essence. How, then, can Marinella maintain the identity of the human species in men and women while asserting the greater nobility of women? There are several ways in which Marinella responds to that objection. The first is implied by the claim that women have a more excellent Idea or Form than men. In a dialogue published some years before the *Nobiltà*, another pro-woman author, Lodovico Domenichi, introduced a character, Francesco Grasso, who argued that women are better than men because the Idea of woman in the mind of God was nobler than the Idea of man.[81] Marinella may then have thought that two persons might have the same species essence while one has a soul that is nobler than the other, because God can choose to transmit to one individual (or one sex) within a species a soul that is the same in kind but nobler in degree. In other words, two souls may be identical in *kind*, but different with respect to the *degree* of nobility they possess. On such a view, the souls of men will have the nobility possessed by every human being in virtue of being the same human essence, but as a sex their souls will have less nobility.

A second response that Marinella makes to the objection that women cannot have nobler souls than men if they are of the same species involves an appeal to the body as an instrument of the soul. There is a precedent, again, for Marinella's view in Domenichi's dialogue, when another character, Lucio Cotto, argues that should we agree that the souls of men and women are the

---

[80] Marinella, *Nobility*, p. 53; trans. modified.
[81] Domenichi, *La nobiltà delle donne*, Bk. I, 9v.

same, then the question becomes whether the *instruments* of the soul are better in one sex; the same point is made in Vincenzo Maggi's *Un brieve trattato dell'eccellentia delle donne* (*A Brief Treatise on the Excellence of Women*) (1545).[82] The instruments of the soul are both the vital spirits that mediate between psychological and physical activity, and the organs of the body. Marinella argues that the female body is physiologically superior to the male in several respects (as we will see in Section 6); one is that women's bodies are better instruments for the activities of the soul. Her view, then, is that women's souls are nobler from the outset, and also that the bodies of women are better at supporting the activities of the soul, which means that those activities are executed in a nobler way. The nobility of a body is not independent of the soul. Rather, on Marinella's account, the greater nobility of women's bodies is a function of their capacity to serve the operations of the soul – to act as excellent instruments for those operations.

We have been discussing Marinella's view of the soul insofar as soul is understood as the rational faculty and identified with intellectual activity. This is because the intellect, or rational faculty, is peculiar to and distinctive of human beings. I have suggested that one way to construe her claim that the souls of women are nobler than the souls of men is to say that the souls of women and men are identical in kind – that is, identical with respect to the essence or form of the human person, the rational faculty – while the souls of women are nobler in degree. The question is whether that nobility attaches exclusively to the rational faculty. While Marinella places emphasis on reason, she acknowledges the existence of other faculties of the soul and elaborates on the claim that women are nobler in part by suggesting that the physiology of women allows the *other* faculties of their souls to operate in a superior way. In the next subsection we will consider how Marinella understands the division of the soul into parts or faculties, and how that understanding underpins her arguments for the nobility of women. We will see that other faculties of the soul, more closely allied to the body than is reason, are also nobler in her view. The upshot is this: that her claim that the souls of women are nobler can be analyzed into two claims: (i) that the rational faculty in women is nobler (i.e. more disposed to virtue), and (ii) that the other faculties of the soul in women are better suited to supporting the rational faculty, for reasons that have to do with the effects of female physiology on the other faculties of soul, as we will see in Section 6.

---

[82] Domenichi, *La nobiltà delle donne*, Bk. II, 56r-v; V. Maggi, *Un brieve trattato*, in S. Plastina, *Mollezza della carne e sotigliezza dell'ingegno: la natura della donna nel Rinascimento europeo* (Rome: Carocci, 2017), pp. 149–50.

5.2 The Divisions of the Soul

In the *Exhortations* Marinella makes explicit that in discussing the soul she is adopting the divisions of the soul established by Aristotle (with some features derived from medieval interpretations of Aristotle):

> The philosopher [i.e. Aristotle] divides the soul into two parts: "*in eam, que habet rationem & in eam, que expers est rationis.*" That is, into one that possesses reason, and another that is without reason. Practical wisdom [*la prudenza*], diligence [*la solertia*], memory, and other things similar to these derive from the rational part of the soul. The part that is not endowed with reason brings forth those things that we say are praiseworthy morally, which we call virtues, such as temperance, fortitude [*fortezza*], justice, and others resembling these, which are praiseworthy in themselves. No one is praised because they are wise or practically wise, but rather for being temperate, just, and strong-minded.[83]

There is an initial division into rational and nonrational parts. In Aristotle's description of the parts of the soul each of these is further subdivided, and those subdivisions are recognized by Marinella.[84] The rational is divided into (i) speculative or theoretical reason, concerned with objects that cannot be otherwise (e.g., essential forms, mathematical objects) and (ii) practical reason, concerned with objects that *can* be otherwise – most notably, our ethical choices and political decisions. This distinction of two parts in the intellect is found also in Dante, who claims that the speculative intellect allows us to reflect upon the works of nature and of God, while the practical intellect governs our actions.[85] The nonrational part of the soul is also subdivided into (i) the nutritive and reproductive faculty which governs physiological function, and is impervious to the influence of reason, and (ii) the desiring part which is responsible for desire, emotion, and "spirit" (an impulse responsible for a range of affects including anger, vengefulness, courage, and affection), which can be influenced by reasoned judgments. In the passage just quoted, Marinella dwells on the division between the rational faculty and the desiring faculty and their respective activities and virtues.

Aristotle distinguished not only the different faculties of the soul, but also the virtues or excellences that belong to the different faculties. There are thus intellectual virtues of both speculative and practical reason: for example, *epistême* or scientific knowledge, and *phronêsis* or practical wisdom (also translated as "prudence"), which is the capacity to recognize the correct course of action and to choose it. Marinella's emphasis lies, however, on the virtues of the desiring faculty of the nonrational soul, usually called the "moral virtues" or

---

[83] Marinella, *Exhortations*, p. 239 (trans. modified); see Aristotle, *Magna Moralia* I.5 1185b1-10; Aristotle, *Nicomachean Ethics* I.13 1102a27.

[84] For Aristotle's division of the soul, see EN I.13 1102a26-1103a3. See also Section 9.2 and n. 228.

[85] Dante, *Convivio* IV: xxii, 11.

"virtues of character," for example, temperance, courage, and justice. On Aristotle's account, the virtues of practical reason and the moral virtues are mutually necessary, so that one cannot be temperate without having practical reasons, and one cannot have practical reason without having all the virtues.[86]

In the *Nobiltà* Marinella does not offer an explicit account of the divisions of the soul, but several of her remarks and arguments suggest that she had in mind the Aristotelian division that she expressly adopts in the *Exhortations*. For example, she says:

> according to the distinction between virtues made by [Torquato Tasso], the speculative part of which he denies is suitable for women. I do not admit this supposition of his. If women are of the same species as men and have the same soul and the same powers, as all the Peripatetics confirm, . . . I would say that speculation is as suitable for women as it is for men.[87]

Her point is that women are as suited to speculative or theoretical reasoning as men, and hence as well able to undertake inquiries into metaphysics or mathematics; implicit in this claim is the distinction between speculative and practical reason. In the same passage Marinella also recognizes practical reason, and argues that Aristotle would grant that women have practical wisdom. We can know this because some women have demonstrated practical wisdom both in military conflicts and in peaceful governance, as well as in the household, all domains that require the exercise of practical reason insofar as they demand decisions for action, both individual and collective.

> I also deny that a woman's practical wisdom (*prudenza*) is obedient to that of her husband, because Aristotle considers a person to be practically wise (*prudente*) who is able to advise and recommend what is best in future matters. Who will deny that there have been many very practically wise (*prudentissime*) women in both military and peacetime administration? Let them read my chapter on practically wise women. And who will deny that women demonstrate great practical wisdom in managing their households? No one, in my opinion.[88]

Marinella then endorses the distinction between speculative and practical reason in the *Nobility*, and insists that women have both capacities, and indeed all the same powers of soul as men.

She also endorses the distinctions between the activities and virtues of the rational faculty and those of the desiring faculty when, for example, she mentions "all the operations of the soul, speculative, practical, and moral."[89] The moral operations of the soul are those desires, decisions and emotions that are associated with the moral virtues and vices. This is most evident in her

---

[86] Aristotle, *EN* VI.3 1144b30-32.   [87] Marinella, *Nobility*, p. 140 (trans. modified).
[88] Marinella, *Nobility*, p. 140; trans. modified.   [89] Marinella, *Nobiltà*, p. 135.

discussion of individual moral virtues in the *Nobility*. For example, in the section on temperate and continent women she begins by saying that "[m]en are called continent and temperate when they use their reason to oppose the delights and pleasures of the senses."[90] That is, to have the virtue of temperance is to experience the correct pleasures to the correct degree, and in that sense to have one's desires under the control of one's reason – to desire as "right reason prescribes."[91] Marinella goes on to argue that, as everyone knows, women are continent and temperate. She attributes, then, to women the intellectual virtues of both speculative and practical reason, and also the moral virtues, and in distinguishing them makes clear that she is assuming the Aristotelian division of the soul into faculties and the distinction among virtues that corresponds to that division.

Moreover, in several passages in the *Nobility* in which Marinella depicts a struggle between the different faculties of the soul she is implicitly, again, endorsing the division of the soul derived from Aristotle's *Nicomachean Ethics*. For example, in the chapter in the second part on incontinent, greedy, drunken, and frenzied men, she notes that incontinence, a moral condition in which one's reasoned judgment is overcome by the desire for pleasure, obscures the intellect, and adds that incontinence renders a man "*imprudente,*" i.e., that it deprives him of practical wisdom.[92] In another chapter of the second part, on angry, strange, and bestial men, she says "anger on most occasions blinds the rational faculty, as we read in [Aristotle's] *Politics* V. 10, and that it obscures the intellect is an undisputed fact."[93] These are both examples of a conflict between some desire of the nonrational part (the desire for physical pleasure, or a "spirited" desire for honor or vengeance) and the judgment of reason, and they rely on the distinction between reason and the desiring part of the soul. We will see that many of Marinella's claims for the superiority of women depend on her assertion that women's desires are more aligned with reason than are the desires of men, and hence that women's souls are better organized and operate more virtuously than the souls of men.

5.3 The Interaction of Soul and Body

We have seen that Marinella asserts that women are superior to men because the souls of women are nobler than men's; that claim has been elaborated in two ways: first, as the assertion that the rational faculty in women is intrinsically nobler from birth, namely that women have a greater or nobler capacity to develop the intellectual virtues, and second, as the assertion that in women the other faculties of the soul (in particular, the desiring faculty) is better aligned

---

[90] Marinella, *Nobility*, p. 93.   [91] Marinella, *Nobility*, p. 93.   [92] Marinella, *Nobiltà*, p. 154.
[93] Marinella, *Nobiltà*, p. 166.

with reason, and hence better able to support the judgments of reason, because of the distinctive character of women's bodies. We will consider that distinctive character in Section 6. Before turning to the body, however, it may be helpful to say something preliminary about Marinella's understanding of the relation of soul to body.

That understanding emerges from the context of her discussion of the causes that bring people into being. Her theory of causation is Aristotelian. She identifies the "efficient or productive cause" of all created beings as God, who, as we have seen in Section 4.1, produces all human beings by transmitting to them an Idea that is both their soul and their species essence.[94] This soul, as the species essence, is the formal cause of a person. As we have just seen in Section 5.2, it is complex, consisting of a rational and a nonrational part. Marinella says that the material cause from which woman was created was "man's rib," alluding to the story of Genesis 2.7 and 2.21–22 in a well-rehearsed argument common to pro-woman contributions to the *querelle*.[95] Since the material cause of men was "mud or mire," women are clearly superior with respect to the material cause as well as the formal cause. The fourth Aristotelian cause is the final cause, the aim or end of something; in both women and men this is beatitude or happiness, the goal of all human activity. From a causal perspective, then, women are the same as men with respect to the efficient and the final cause, but superior with respect to the formal and material cause, namely with respect to body and soul.

In the fully formed person, the formal cause (the soul) and the material cause (the body) interact, or should interact, in a variety of ways. In particular, Marinella says that the soul "commands" the body, but also that the soul is "dependent" on the body.

> Women, like men, consist of two parts. One, the origin and principle of all noble deeds, is referred to by everyone as the soul. The other part is the transitory and mortal body, which is obedient to the commands of the soul, just as the soul is dependent on the body.[96]

The soul commands the body in a particular sense: the rational soul determines and constrains (at least ideally) the desires that arise from sensory experience, namely from the body. In a complete, mature, and virtuous person, the rational faculty decides which desires conform to its judgments, and hence which to sanction and encourage. Since those desires emerge from our embodied experience, the soul commands the body, and the rational faculty commands the faculty of desire, which, while nonrational, is susceptible to

---

[94] Marinella, *Nobility*, p. 52.   [95] Marinella, *Nobility*, p. 54.   [96] Marinella, *Nobility*, p. 55.

reason in a way that the lowest faculty of soul, the reproductive/nutritive faculty, is not. In what sense, then, is the soul "dependent" on the body? In the next section I consider how Marinella understands the physiology of the sexed body to influence the capacities of soul and the opportunities for virtue.

6 Physiology

6.1 Introduction

Although Marinella's claim for the superiority of women assigns nobility primarily to the soul, several of her arguments centre on the female body, and its superiority to the male. This, as I have suggested in Section 5, is because Marinella views the body as an instrument of the soul that may be better or less well adapted to the operations of the soul (i.e. reasoning, remembering, desiring). Thus one human body is nobler than another when it is better suited to the execution of human activities, all of which are, or should be, guided by reason. So while a body can be more or less noble, that nobility is a function of its capacity to support the soul.

Marinella's understanding of the differences between the bodies of men and women is derived from contemporary medical and biological accounts, which were much influenced by ancient medicine in both the Hippocratic and Galenic traditions, and the natural philosophy of Aristotle. These accounts focus less on the roles played by male and female in the generation of offspring, and more on the underlying physiology of the body. To follow Marinella's reasoning in claiming that the female body is better suited to support reason and to keep desire under the control of the rational faculty we need to consider the context of sixteenth-century medicine and the biology of Aristotle.

6.2 The Medical Context

Two factors made contemporary medical knowledge available to Marinella: her access to the libraries of her father, her brother, and her husband, all of whom were physicians, and her knowledge of Latin, in which most (although not all) medical texts of the period were written. Most physicians in the sixteenth century identified as followers of Galen, but there were other ancient influences on medicine: the biology of Aristotle, the works of Avicenna, and the newly rediscovered Hippocratic texts (translated into Latin in 1525), the study of which produced humanist physicians, interested in the questions raised by the medical texts of antiquity, freed from scholastic interpretation.[97] Because Galen

---

[97] I. Maclean, *The Renaissance Notion of Woman: A Study in the Fortunes of Scholasticism and Medical Science in European Intellectual Life* (Cambridge: Cambridge University Press, 1980), p. 28.

represented himself as an interpreter of Hippocrates, and because his medicine drew on the familiar philosophies of Plato and of Aristotle, Galenic–Hippocratic medicine came to predominate in the sixteenth century.[98] At the same time, the growth of experimental anatomy allowed physicians to confirm or contest ancient accounts of the structure of the body, its physiology, the illnesses to which it was subject, and therapeutic remedies.[99] Renaissance authors, like medieval authors, did not always cite the sources of their opinions and felt free to borrow from both learned works and popular views, so that the source of a claim, or the evidence for it, is sometimes obscure.[100]

The influence of Galenic–Hippocratic medicine on the discussion of women's physiology and complexion is clear; it was a source for both pro-woman and misogynist claims. Physicians emphasized the importance of maintaining or restoring balance in a number of respects: balance among the principles of hot and cold, wet and dry, and more concretely balance among the humors (cholera, phlegm, black bile, and blood). Both Aristotle and Galen believed the female was physiologically colder than the male, and heat was usually associated with the male in Hippocratic treatises (although *Diseases of Women I* suggests that women are hotter than men, so there was disagreement on this point even among Hippocratics).[101] Galen and the Hippocratic authors assumed that both the male and female parent contributed "seed" to the process of conception, and hence provided some support to pro-woman authors who wanted to argue for the agency of women in generation.[102] At the same time, the prevailing conception of women as colder and weaker than men, and the emphasis that Hippocratic authors placed on the uterus as an organ that disposed women to experience strong sexual desires, was used by misogynist authors to depict women as innately lascivious.[103]

The translation of the Hippocratic works, including their gynecological treatises, contributed to a trend toward a more specialized literature on the

---

[98] Vivian Nutton, "God, Galen and the Depaganization of Ancient Medicine, in *Religion and Medicine in the Middle Ages*, P. Biller and J. Ziegler (eds.) (York: York Medieval Press, 2001), pp. 23–24; Nutton has much more to say about how pagan medicine came to be acceptable in Christian contexts.

[99] Maclean, *Renaissance Notion*, pp. 28–29.

[100] J. Cadden, *Meanings of Sex Difference in the Middle Ages: Medicine, Science, and Culture*, (Cambridge: Cambridge University Press, 1993), p. 12.

[101] Aristotle, GA IV. 1 766a31-7; Galen, *Temp.* II 606 Kühn (in Galen, *Works on Human Nature*, Vol. 1 *Mixtures (De temperamentis)*, P. N. Singer and Philip J. van der Eijk (eds.) [Cambridge: Cambridge University Press, 2018] p. 128). Hippocrates and E. Littré. *Oeuvres Complètes d'Hippocrate*, vol. 4 (Paris: J.B. Baillière, 1839–61), pp. 12–13.

[102] On the debate about female "seed," see McLean, *Renaissance Notion*, pp. 35–37.

[103] See H. King, *Hippocrates' Woman: Reading the Female Body in Ancient Greece* (New York: Routledge, 1998), pp. 33–36 on the uterus in Hippocratic texts, and pp. 222–225 on the depiction in Plato's *Timaeus* of the uterus as a living animal.

diseases of women.[104] The rise of gynecology in the Renaissance was powered not only by an interest in works *about* women, but also by a demand for works addressed *to* women, as midwives and as patients.[105] Some physicians began publishing medical works in the vernacular on obstetrical issues, aimed primarily at an audience of literate midwives.[106] This literature is characterized not only by a concern for the physiology and ailments of women, but also by a pro-woman attitude, motivated by the existence of an elite class seeking better medical care for women, a growing interest among the reading public for material on sexuality and reproduction, and competition for the patronage of women with political power.[107]

This pro-woman attitude in much medical literature of the period was manifest especially in arguments against the view that women are anatomically or physiologically inferior to men, often attributed to Aristotle in its origins. Aristotle had maintained, as we have seen, the unity of the species by arguing that the sexes were the same in kind; Marinella, like many pro-woman authors, relied on Aristotle's authority in claiming the same rational capacity for women and men. At the same time, however, Aristotle had claimed that female nature was, "as it were, a deformity,"[108] a claim that was interpreted in the Renaissance to mean that women were somehow imperfect or incomplete, and the misogynist tracts of the sixteenth century highlighted that aspect of Aristotle's biology.[109] The medical writers denied the inferiority of women, rejecting not only Aristotle's claim that the female is imperfect in certain respects relative to the male but also more general misogynist stereotypes of the female as inferior.[110] By the second half of the sixteenth century most authors of gynecological texts had moved away from conceiving of women as imperfect men to the view that each sex was perfect as such, with an equally important role to play in generation.[111] Pro-woman authors followed suit, arguing that men and women are equally perfect with respect to their essential form, despite any differences in anatomy or physiology. Arguments for the worth of women in the sixteenth century were thus aligned with much of contemporary medical opinion.[112]

---

[104] Pomata, "Was There a Querelle," pp. 323–324; Cadden, *Meanings of Sex Difference*, p. 16.
[105] Pomata, "Was There a Querelle," p. 332.
[106] Pomata, "Was There a Querelle," p. 323, 336–337.
[107] Pomata, "Was There a Querelle," p. 338.   [108] Aristotle, *GA* VI.4 775a15-16.
[109] MacLean, *Renaissance Notion*, pp. 30–33.
[110] MacLean, *Renaissance Notion*, pp. 29–30; Pomata, "Was There a Querelle," p. 332.
[111] Pomata, "Was There a Querelle," p. 335; MacLean, *Renaissance Notion*, p. 29.
[112] Pomata, "Was There a Querelle," p. 317; against this view see M. Bolufer, "Medicine and the *Querelle des Femmes* in Early Modern Spain," *Medical History*, 29 (2009), 86–106.

In this context of renewed interest in the bodily manifestation of sexual difference, a number of philosophical issues concerned with that difference were the focus of discussion. (i) One fundamental question was whether male and female should be conceived as identical in species, or rather as different kinds. Although virtually all participants agreed on the human status of women, some suggested that women were similar to animals.[113] (ii) A second issue concerned a set of questions about the uterus: Was it an independent animal? Did it desire the male? Did it produce special psychological effects in women? (iii) A third issue connected physiological claims with moral and social concerns: did the relative coldness of women's bodies (a fact almost universally accepted) render them somehow inferior to men intellectually or morally?[114] All of these were questions that could be found in ancient medical and philosophical texts, which suggests that the debate about the nature and qualities of women in the Renaissance phase of the *querelle des femmes* was structured around concerns at the intersections of medicine and natural, moral, and political philosophy.

Marinella, as we have seen in Sections 4 and 5, was interested in the first question, and developed her own nuanced and unusual response, agreeing that the sexes were the same in kind, while also arguing that, nonetheless, they had different degrees of nobility. She was also particularly interested in the third; I explore her position on that question in the next subsection. And we can see intimations of a concern with the second question in her discussion of beauty and desire; we will consider that in Section 7.

6.3 The Aristotelian Context

While the influence of contemporary medical opinion created a climate in which more favourable attitudes to the female body were taken seriously, in Marinella's treatment of sexual difference as a physiological phenomenon it is Aristotle primarily to whom she refers, both to support her fundamental claim about physiological difference and to contest his claims about the implications of that difference. Since references to Aristotle's biology often figured in the misogynist literature in support of the claim that the female body was imperfect,

---

[113] For example, G. Passi, *I donneschi difetti* (Venezia, 1599); anonymous pamphlet entitled *Che le donne non siano della stessa specie degli uomini* – sometimes attributed to Giovan Francesco Loredan, founder of the Accademia degli Incogniti – circulating in Latin from 1595 and published in Italian translation two years after the *Essortationi*, in 1647 (see L. Panizza, "Introduction," in A. Tarabotti, *Paternal Tyranny* [Chicago: University of Chicago Press, 2004] pp. 11–12) and E. B. Weaver, "Introduction" in A. Tarabotti, E. B. Weaver (ed. and trans.), *Antisatire: In Defense of Women, against Franceco Buoninsegni* (New York/Toronto: Iter Press, 2020).

[114] See Maclean, *Renaissance Notion*, pp. 34, 38.

Marinella's use of Aristotle, and her criticisms of him, are intended to contest the interpretations and the conclusions of misogynists. Although "[m]isogyny and Scholastic Aristotelianism fused in the eyes of humanist physicians into a single object of rejection and scorn," Marinella sought both to reject the misogyny in Aristotelianism, and to preserve the philosophical claims and arguments that would support the pro-woman cause.[115] She was able to do this in part because neo-Aristotelians of the period did not concur in their interpretations of Aristotle; Marinella exploits the ambiguity of some of Aristotle's claims about sexual difference.[116] Since Aristotle attributed the physiological inferiority of the female to the coldness of her body, and since a difference in temperature in the body was widely accepted among Renaissance physicians and philosophers who addressed questions of sexual difference, let us begin with an overview of the claims about temperature in Aristotle's works insofar as they might be supposed to affect the character of the sexes.

Aristotle, following some Hippocratic authors, claims that the male, especially in human beings, is hotter than the female;[117] this heat is responsible for the more complete concoction of blood into semen. He states clearly both (i) that the character of blood affects many things, and (ii) that temperature is a key feature of that character, in a passage from the *Parts of Animals*:

> The nature of the blood is the cause of many features of animals with respect to both character and perception, as is reasonable, since blood is the matter of the entire body ... It therefore makes a great difference whether it is hot or cold, thin or thick, turbid or pure.[118]

Aristotle specifies what the considerable differences are in the *Parts of Animals* when he says at II.4 650b19-22 that some animals have a more subtle intelligence not because of the coldness of their blood, but because they have thin and pure blood, and explains this by saying that animals with "finer and purer moisture have quicker perception." So thin, pure blood leads to quicker perception, which in turn leads to a subtler intelligence. Aristotle associates thin, pure blood with heat, intelligence, and male animals in another passage from the *Parts of Animals*.[119]

In the *Generation of Animals* this account is refined somewhat, when Aristotle says that the intelligence of an animal may be due not simply to the purity of the blood, but more precisely to the purity *of the heat* in the heart that is

[115] Pomata, "Was There a Querelle," p. 339.

[116] On disagreements among neo-Aristotelian physicians, see McLean, *Renaissance Notion*, p. 36.

[117] Aristotle, *GA*, IV.6 775a6-8.

[118] Aristotle, *Parts of Animals*, J. G. Lennox (trans.) (Oxford: Oxford University Press, 2001), II.4 651a12-17.

[119] Aristotle, *PA* II. 2 648a9-13; Lennox (trans. modified).

transmitted to the blood: "the heat in the heart is purest in people. The blend (*eukrasian*) [of hot and cold] is shown by the possession of intellect: of animals people are the most intelligent."[120]

Aristotle's position has shifted: intelligence is now associated with a blend of hot and cold in the heart (and hence in the blood), rather than with hot blood. In both this passage and the one from the *Parts of Animals* the word "intelligence" and its cognates translate *phronêsis*, which is the term Aristotle uses for the virtue of practical wisdom, required in all matters of political and moral deliberation.[121] This discussion, and especially this last passage from the *Generation of Animals*, prove to be important for Marinella's case for the superiority of women.

In his practical philosophy, encompassing moral and political theory, Aristotle also traces a connection between heat and certain traits that affect the character. *Thumos*, which is generally translated as "temper," "spiritedness," or "passion," is one kind of desire (see *De anima* II.3 414b1-2). Aristotle treats it as a nonrational desire, often for honor, and sees it as a source of anger and also of a primitive form of courage. It is associated with male animals at *History of Animals* IX.1 608a33-35, and with heat and masculine activities, in the *Nicomachean Ethics* at VII.6 1149a25-34:

> [*Thumos*] in such cases seems to hear what reasons says, but to mishear it, like hasty servants who run out of the room before they have heard everything . . . just so a hot and quick nature means that temper [*thumos*] hears – but does not hear the order, before rushing to vengeance. For reason, or sensory appearances, indicate "unprovoked aggression" or "insult," and *thumos*, as if having reasoned it out that this sort of thing is cause for going to war, moves into angry mode at once.[122]

This description of *thumos* as hot, hasty, moving immediately to anger and hence uncontrolled are used by Marinella to argue that men are morally inferior to women because of their physiology. She may have been drawing on contemporary Aristotelian sources, such as Jacopo of Forlì, who, in his *De generatione embrionis* said that "it must be noted that male differs from female in three [ways], namely complexion, disposition, and shape. And among these complexion is the most fundamental."[123]

---

[120] Aristotle, *Generation of Animals*, A. L. Peck (trans.) (Cambridge, MA: Harvard University Press, 1942), II.6 744a29-32; trans. modified.

[121] Aristotle, *EN*, VI.1 1139a5-8; see also Section 7.1.

[122] Aristotle, *Nicomachean Ethics*. C. J. Rowe and S. Broadie (trans.) (Oxford: Oxford University Press, 2002), trans. modified.

[123] Fol. 9vb, cited by Cadden, *Meanings of Sex Difference*, p. 170.

6.4 Marinella on Female Physiology

Viewed against the background of the Renaissance reception of ancient medicine and Aristotle's biology, we can recognize the ways in which Marinella both appropriated and elaborated arguments from physiology to defend women – arguments that had often been deployed in attacks on the worth of women. In the misogynistic literature of the period, women were said to be colder than men on the authority of Aristotle and Galen, and to be morally and intellectually inferior as a result of their colder nature. This association (often undeveloped) of bodily temperature and psychological features was forged in part through the concept of "complessione" ("complexion" or "temperament"), which referred to the character or constitution of an individual or of a kind.[124] Marinella appeals explicitly to the complexion of women as evidence for the superiority of her body: "The greater nobility and worthiness of a woman's body is shown by its delicacy, its complexion, and its temperate nature."[125] The physical character of a person's body was described in the Aristotelian tradition and in Hippocratic and Galenic medicine, as hot or cold, and wet or dry. Temperature was thus only one aspect of the constitution, although it was often used synecdochally to stand for the bodily constitution as a whole. Moreover, the term "complessione" could signify the moral as well as the physical constitution of a person, which allowed for some ambiguity and overlap between the notion of a physical character and that of a moral character. In that context we find the suggestion that the physical constitution of a sex might inform or even determine the psychological traits of a character.

Marinella claims, as we have seen, that a woman's soul is nobler than a man's; we can know that because "the nobility of the soul can be judged from the excellence of the body."[126] She often appeals to the bodies of women as evidence for their superiority, whether she argues that their bodies are signs of that superiority (as in the case of beauty – see Section 7) or rather causes of it (as in the case of the complexion). Marinella's contention is founded on an important point of agreement with Aristotle, at least initially: that men are hotter than women. She also agrees with him, and others, that the temperature of the body has significant consequences for the worth of a person: "virtues and defects of the body depend on its temperature, which, if excessive, causes reason to be overcome."[127] Despite these agreements, she arrives at the

---

[124] On the development of the theory of temperaments, see Jacques Jouanna, "The Legacy of the Hippocratic Treatise *The Nature of Man*: The Theory of the Four Humours" in J. Jouanna, *Greek Medicine from Hippocrates to Galen: Selected Papers*, Philip van der Eijk (ed.), Neil Allies (trans.) (Leiden: Brill, 2012), 335–359.

[125] Marinella, *Nobility*, p. 57.   [126] Marinella, *Nobility*, p. 57.   [127] Marinella, *Nobility*, p. 77.

conclusion that women are superior to men by arguing that men are *excessively* hot and that a high degree of heat is not beneficial to human activity.

First, Marinella points out that temperature is a relative notion, so that to say that women are colder than men is not to say necessarily that they are cold in absolute terms. In fact, she contends, women are cooler than men in the sense that they are of a moderate temperature whereas men are excessively hot. In other words, it is not that women are too cold, but rather that men are too hot.[128] This is a point that Castiglione had made: il Magnifico says "I say to you that woman is of a cold temperament [*complession frigida*] in comparison with man, who by excess of warmth is far from temperate; but woman, taken in herself, is temperate ... because the moisture she has in her is proportionate to her natural warmth, which in man more readily evaporates and is consumed because of excessive dryness."[129]

Marinella then depicts the moderate temperature of women as the cause of various psychological benefits, and as a corollary, the hotter temperature of the bodies of men as the cause of their many debilities and vices. She is helped in this by Aristotle's assertion at *Generation of Animals* II.6 744a29-32 (quoted earlier) that it is a *blend* of hot and cold that is best. Marinella asserts, citing Plutarch as her authority, that "heat is an instrument of the soul."[130] That is, the activities of the soul operate through the mechanism of heat, and those activities include the varieties of reason (practical and theoretical), desire, and decision-making. Citing Ficino, she adds that it is not that all heat is good for the soul's activities; it must be the *correct* degree of heat. "[L]ittle and failing heat, as in old people, is completely powerless (*impotentissimo*) for the soul's operations," but it is also true that excessive heat "makes souls precipitous (*precipitose*) and unbridled (*sfrenate*)."[131] A certain mean between too little and too much heat in the body is then optimal for allowing the soul to carry out its activities, and the female body manifests this mean.

What, then are the effects of moderate vital heat in a woman's body? Marinella denies that greater heat makes one nobler.[132] This is because "[a hot and dry constitution] causes and produces an infinite number of ill effects (such as more passionate appetites and uncontrolled desires) that a moderate heat does not provoke."[133] We must look to her predecessors to fill out the argument that a temperate bodily constitution best serves the activities of the soul.

First, pro-woman authors argued that there were intellectual advantages women obtained from having a colder body temperature. Some misogynists

---

128 Marinella, *Nobility*, p. 130.   129 Castiglione, *The Courtier*, p. 219.
130 Marinella, *Nobility*, p. 130.   131 Marinella, *Nobility*, p. 130; Marinella, *Nobiltà*, p. 119.
132 Marinella, *Nobility*, p. 130.   133 Marinella, *Nobiltà*, p. 136.

had suggested that a colder temperature had the effect of rendering one's sensory impressions imperfect or obscured, drawing on Aristotle's suggestion that the nature of the blood affected perception, and assuming that deleterious effects on perception would ultimately yield a compromised understanding.[134] Castiglione had argued, on the contrary, that women might have "more fixed impressions from her coldness,"[135] calling into question that the effect of a lower temperature on the blood would be one that led to uncertain or varying impressions. And in Lodovico Domenichi's dialogue *La nobiltà delle donne* (*The Nobility of Women*) (1551) one character offers an account that resembles Castiglione's: heat, by thinning the blood in which sense impressions are formed, leads to less firm impressions and hence to a less reliable intelligence.[136] There are precedents, then, for Marinella's claim that a more moderate temperature, as in the bodies of women, is better for the speculative and practical operations of reason.

Another way in which some pro-woman authors thought that body temperature might affect intelligence was indirectly, through its effects on the emotions and desires. For example, Capra, in *Eccellenza e dignità delle donne* (*The Virtue and Dignity of Women*) (1525) conceded that women were colder than men, and that it was a necessary and invariable difference between the sexes.[137] He conceded further that women were less "quick" intellectually as a result of this coldness. His argument in defense of the capacities of women was that the higher temperature of men's bodies affected them in emotional and moral ways that interfered with the exercise of their intellectual capacities, with the result that men manifested less practical wisdom than women. To arrive at that conclusion, Capra drew on the association Aristotle had posited of heat with *thumos* (spiritedness), a desire for honor or a disposition to anger. He claimed that the natural heat of men disposed them to anger, while the natural coldness of women protected them from it. Anger, on his account, is an emotion that disturbs a person, making them less rational and less able to act in a calm and considered manner. The higher temperature of the male body then causes men to be more often and easily overcome by anger and violent impulses, because heat produces *thumos*, which gives rise to irrational violence.[138] Since practical wisdom depends on having the passions under the control of reason, men are less likely to be practically wise even though they are by nature more quick-witted. This is the sort of view that Marinella seems to have in mind when she

---

[134] See Aristotle, *On Memory*, 450a26-b8 for the suggestion that imperfect perception will affect memory. See also M. Leunissen, *From Natural Character to Moral Virtue in Aristotle* (Oxford University Press, 2017), pp. 153–154.

[135] See Castiglione, *The Courtier*, p. 218.   [136] Domenichi, *La nobiltà delle donne*, 18v.

[137] Capra, *Eccellenza*, pp. 75–76.   [138] Capra, *Eccellenza*, p. 75.

says that the hot and dry complexion of men leads them to have "more passionate appetites and uncontrolled desires." She diverges, however, from Capra's position in refusing to allow that the greater heat of men provides any intellectual advantage. On the contrary, she asserts that the moderate temperature of the female body makes women rational in a firm and unwavering way at the same time that it renders them temperate with respect to pleasure and honour. So she concludes that there are moral as well as intellectual advantages to the cooler, more moderate constitution of women.

For Marinella, then, the deleterious effects of excessive vital heat were multiple. The heat of the male body rendered men intellectually superficial by making the blood thinner, more fluid, and hence less able to retain sense impressions. Moreover, a hot constitution made a person excessive with respect both to the appetites (desires for physical pleasure) and to *thumos* (desire for honor), which in turn led to two consequences. First, since reason could be overcome by excessive desires of either sort, when heat produced excessive appetites or thumotic desires, it obstructed the operation of reason. Marinella established that the pleasures of the senses obscure the intellect, and offered as examples a number of men who were excessive in physical pleasures or in anger, with the result that their reason was impaired.[139] Second, these excessive appetites and thumotic desires themselves constituted moral failings, so that a hotter body led men to have more vicious moral characters. In other words, because men are excessively hot, and excessive heat diminishes one's intellectual capacities while augmenting the irrational passions to the degree that they are able to overwhelm the judgments of reason, men are rendered morally and intellectually incompetent by their physiology.

In this argument Marinella seems to accept that there are consistent differences in vital heat between men and women, from which she argues for the superiority of women. But she also offers arguments that seem to contest the assumption of such consistent differences by considering (i) variations according to the stage of life or geographic locations, and (ii) individual exceptions. She says that women in Africa or Spain are hotter than men who live "in the cold north, or in Germany."[140] She is, I suspect, noticing a tension in ancient claims about sexual differences in vital heat and accounts of the interaction of warmer climates on the character of people living in those climates. Such accounts occur in works in the Hippocratic corpus (*Airs, Waters, Places* 23–24), and in Aristotle (*Politics* VII.7 1327b19-37), but it is not clear how climactic effects on vital heat are supposed to affect, or not affect, the vital heat that on these accounts is natural to the sexes. If moving from one region to another might make a woman hotter than men in a different region, then women are not colder

---

[139] Marinella, *Nobiltà*, pp. 154, 155–156, 166.   [140] Marinella, *Nobility*, p. 131.

than men by nature, but only contingently, and so the basis of the argument from physiology is undermined. Moreover, she claims, there are certainly people who have natures that are hotter than the nature of Plato or Aristotle.[141] The point of this claim is that there will be variations in the bodily temperature of individuals within the same sex, and that those variations will not correlate with intellectual capacities; she is not saying that some individuals are more brilliant than Plato or Aristotle, but that no one could be ("And are their spirits therefore nobler? Indeed!"[142]). If that is true, and yet some people are hotter than these philosophers, then it must be the case that the degree of vital heat a person possesses is not a measure of the intelligence of that person. Again, this seems to undermine the argument from physiology.

Yet Marinella's conclusion to the discussion of vital heat once again endorses the idea that the relative coolness of women's bodies is an advantage:

> Let us therefore say this, that women are cooler than men and thus nobler, and that if a man performs excellent deeds it is because his nature is similar to a woman's possessing temperate but not excessive heat, and because his years of virile maturity have tempered the fervor of that heat he possessed in his youth and made his nature more feminine so that it operates with greater wisdom and maturity.[143]

Once again the argument depends on ancient views, in this case about temperature variations that track age so that older bodies are colder and younger bodies hotter.[144] Marinella draws a parallel that ancient authors do not, between the degree of vital heat in an older man's body and the degree of heat in a woman's body, where both are contrasted with the degree of heat in a younger man's body. Her point is that older men are physiologically similar to women, which is why they have greater wisdom and maturity (i.e. less moral recklessness). So Marinella offers a two-pronged argument against the view that the coldness of women is a disadvantage: she argues both (i) that women are colder, and that coldness is an advantage, and (ii) that if women are *not* colder, as suggested by individual variations over location and age, the view is nonsense.

7 Beauty

7.1 Introduction

As we saw in Section 6, while Marinella's central claim is that women are superior to men with respect to their souls, she argues that superiority of soul is enabled and supported by the *physiology* of the female body. Another of her

---

[141] Marinella, *Nobility*, p. 131.   [142] Marinella, *Nobility*, p. 131.
[143] Marinella, *Nobility*, p. 131.   [144] Aristotle, *De Longitudine et Brevitate Vitae* 466a 17–23.

arguments, the focus of this section, is that the *beauty* of women's bodies is a sign or manifestation of the nobility of their souls.[145] This is not a self-evident claim. In order to understand the relation Marinella posits between the nobility of the soul and the beauty that she takes to be characteristic of women, we need to consider both her argument from beauty and the sources she drew on to formulate it. The argument is found in Chapter Three of Part One of the *Nobility*, "Of the Nature and Essence of the Female Sex," which follows immediately on the conclusion that the souls of women are superior to those of men (see Section 4). While its point of departure is a claim about the beauty of the bodies of women, the substance of the argument concerns their souls. In this section we will consider the argument from beauty to intellectual and moral superiority, the context in which that argument was possible, Marinella's adaptation and development of her sources, and the ways in which her views on beauty shift between the *Nobiltà* and the *Essortationi*.

7.2 Beauty as Metaphysical, Epistemological, and Moral

In the *Nobiltà* Marinella conceives of beauty as a "grace" or "splendor" or "ray of light" that emanates from the soul and infuses the body, tracing this conception to Plotinus[146] and ultimately to Plato:

> the nobility of the soul can be judged from the excellence of the body – which is ornamented with the same character and beauty as the soul, "which such a body manifests in itself." The greater nobility and worthiness of a woman's body is shown by its delicacy, its complexion, and its temperate nature, as well as by its beauty, which is a grace or splendor proceeding from the soul as well as from the body. Beauty is without doubt a ray of light from the soul that pervades the body in which it finds itself.[147]

She claims that "[t]he soul . . . is the cause and origin of physical beauty" and that "God, the stars, the sky, nature, love and the elements are the origin and source of beauty" because beauty "is dependent on the supernal light."[148] The beauty of women's bodies is thus a kind of grace that manifests as light emanating from their souls, which derives ultimately from its origin in the divine. In arguing that beauty cannot "come solely from the body" Marinella remarks that "[b]eauty and majesty of body are . . . born of superior reason."[149] So she attributes the beauty of women's bodies to the superiority of their souls, and more specifically to the superiority *of the rational faculty*. This suggests that

---

[145] Marinella, *Nobility*, p. 55.
[146] Plotinus, *The Essential Plotinus: Representative Treatises from the Enneads*, E. J. O'Brien (trans.) (Indianapolis: Hackett Publishing, 1964), V.8.3.
[147] Marinella, *Nobility*, p. 57.   [148] Marinella, *Nobility*, p. 58.   [149] Marinella, *Nobility*, p. 59.

her claim, discussed in Sections 4 and 5, that women's souls are better than men's implies that women possess a better faculty of reason.

Marinella pursues the idea that the physical beauty of women is a manifestation of a divine light by elaborating on the causal links between God and women:

> I would not merely call beauty a staircase. I believe it to be the golden chain referred to by Homer that can always raise minds toward God and can never, for any reason, be dragged down toward earth. This is because beauty, not being earthly but divine and celestial, always raises us toward God, from whom it is derived. This is shown in the following lines by Petrarch:
>
> "From one beauty to another I raise myself gazing on the first cause"
>
> This means, "I ascend from beauty to beauty," that is, from link to link, "and I base myself on the first cause." The first link of our golden chain that, descending from heaven, gently carries away our souls, is corporeal beauty. This is gazed at and considered by the mind, through means of the outer eye, which enjoys and finds moderate pleasure in it, but then, conquered by supreme sweetness, ascends to the second link and contemplates and gazes with the internal eye at the soul that, adorned with celestial excellence, gives form to the beautiful body. Not stopping at this second beauty or link, but avid and desirous of a more vivid beauty and almost inflamed by love, the mind ascends to the third link, in order to compare earthly and celestial beauties and raise itself to heaven. From there it contemplates the angelic spirits, and finally this contemplative mind seats itself within the great light of the angels, and thus of the one who supports the chain. So the soul, taking delight in Him, is made happy and blessed.[150]

In this passage there are, implicitly or explicitly, three ideas concerned with beauty: (i) that beauty is a sign of the metaphysical superiority of women – the superiority of their nature or being, (ii) that beauty gives women an epistemological advantage over men, making the contemplation of the divine more easily accessible to women, and (iii) that the beauty of women can explain what Marinella sees as the gap between the desire that men experience for women, and the absence of desire women feel for men. In Subsections 7.3–7.5 I consider Marinella's discussion of each of these ideas, and the philosophical sources she drew from, to render her argument with greater clarity and precision, and to demonstrate how she was able to make novel use of familiar philosophical texts to defend the worth of women. She was relying on certain commonplaces of the period: the view that women are beautiful and men are not; that a respectable woman will not experience sexual desire; that God is the creator of all beings.

---

[150] Marinella, *Nobility*, p. 66.

But her argument is primarily a philosophical one, drawing from a range of sources, both ancient and contemporary.

7.3 Beauty as Metaphysical

The metaphor of "the golden chain of Homer," as it was elaborated by later authors, refers to the series of different kinds of beings, with different degrees of worth, that constitute the cosmos.[151] It is the centerpiece of Marinella's discussion of beauty, and the focus of the metaphysical claim to superiority. In Marinella's description the lowest link in the chain is "corporeal beauty," the next is "the soul . . . that gives form to the beautiful body," and the next after that is celestial beauty, followed by "angelic spirits." In employing the metaphor Marinella is emphasizing the intrinsic differences in worth in the sexes as objects of love, since the links in the golden chain represent different kinds, arranged hierarchically from best (the highest link on the chain) to worst (the lowest). She identifies "corporeal beauty" with women, which marks them off as the lowest of the links mentioned; but men are, apparently, a link below women on the chain. Since women are higher in the chain that ends with God and the Good itself, they are closer to God and of greater intrinsic worth than men.

This interpretation of Homer's golden chain emerged in later Platonism from a passage in Plato's *Timaeus* in which he suggests that all possible kinds are realized (the "principle of plenitude"),[152] together with a passage from Aristotle's *History of Animals* that describes the different kinds of being, inanimate and animate, as existing on a continuum (the "principle of continuity").[153] In combining these two principles an understanding of the structure of the universe emerged in medieval and Renaissance philosophy, according to which it was

> a "Great Chain of Being," composed of an immense, or . . . of an infinite, number of links ranging in hierarchical order from the meagerest kind of existents . . . through "every possible" grade up to the *ens perfectissimum* – or . . . to the highest possible kind of creature.. every one of them differing from that immediately above and that immediately below it by the "least possible" degree of difference.[154]

The identification of this hierarchy of beings with Homer's golden chain came through Macrobius' commentary on Cicero's *Dream of Scipio* (itself much influenced by Plotinus), in which Macrobius writes:

---

[151] Homer, *Illiad* 8.1, 19–22.   [152] Plato, *Timaeus* 29e-31a; see also Plato, *Parmenides* 130c.
[153] Aristotle, *HA* VIII.1 588b4-12.
[154] A. O. Lovejoy, *The Great Chain of Being* (Cambridge: Harvard University Press, 1936), p. 59.

> Since, from the Supreme God Mind arises, and from Mind, Soul, and since
> this in turn creates all subsequent things and fills them all with life, and since
> this single radiance illumines all and is reflected in each ... and since all
> things follow in continuous succession, degenerating in sequence to the very
> bottom of the series, the attentive observer will discover a connection of parts,
> from the Supreme God down to the last dregs of things, mutually linked
> together and without a break. And this is Homer's golden chain, which God,
> he says, bade hang down from heaven to earth.[155]

This conception of the golden chain appears in other Platonists in late antiquity
and into the medieval period.[156] It was widespread in Renaissance philosophy
and literature, for example in the work of Giordano Bruno.[157]

The foundation of this conception, on which Marinella's argument from
beauty relies, is the metaphysics of Plotinus, who posited a first principle, the
One, from which other principles "emanate" or "flow": Intellect, Soul, and
Matter.[158] The One is a cause in the sense that it is virtually everything else, and
everything derives from it in an "atemporal ontological dependence."[159] That is,
the later principles in the sequence are ontologically dependent on the earlier –
posterior in that sense. The Intellect is identified by commentators with both the
set of Platonic Forms or Ideas and with Aristotle's unmoved or first mover; so
the Intellect is both the source of the forms or essences of all things, and the final
cause toward which everything is inclined. The series of principles thus both
describes a scale of value, and also traces a path one can follow to the
knowledge of the One, or God.

Marinella may also have had in mind Augustine's conception of beauty:
something is both good and beautiful when its essential form has impressed
itself completely on its matter, namely when its essential form (its soul) is fully
realized in the appropriate matter.[160] Like Plotinus, Augustine suggests that
God has ordered created beings on a scale of sorts, from visible to invisible,
from mortal to immortal. When we regard the scale and see that it is beautiful,

---

[155] Macrobius, *Commentarii in somnium Scipionis* I, 14, 15, quoted in Lovejoy, *The Great Chain*,
p. 63.

[156] For evidence of the golden chain in Proclus and in Michael Psellos, see P. Lévêque, *Aurea
catena Homeri: une etude sur l'allégorie Grecque* (*Annales Littéraires De L'université De
Besancon* Vol. 27/ Paris: Les Belles Lettres, 1959), pp. 61–65 and 77–81. For more on
Marinella's Platonist influences, see Marco Piana, "Divinae Pulchritudinis Imago: The
Neoplatonic Construction of Female Identity in Lucrezia Marinella's *La nobiltà et l'eccellenze
delle donne* (1601)," in *Genealogie. Re-Writing the Canon: Women Writing in XVI–XVII
Century Italy* (Seville: Arcibel 2018), pp. 199–221, and Peter Adamson, "The Reception of
Plato on Women: Proclus, Averroes, Marinella," in K. R. O'Reilly and C. Pellò (eds.), *Ancient
Women Philosophers: Recovered Ideas and New Perspectives* (Cambridge: Cambridge
University Press, 2023), pp. 241–45.

[157] Lovejoy, *The Great Chain*, pp. 116–121.   [158] Plotinus, *Enneads* V.2.1.

[159] L. Gerson, "Plotinus," in E. N. Zalta (ed.), *Stanford Encyclopedia of Philosophy*, section 2.

[160] St. Augustine, *De vera religione*, 20, 40; P.L. 34 cols. 138–139.

we are led to God.[161] The purpose of the beauty of sensible objects, on Augustine's account, is to make God known to us; because beauty derives from God, it also constitutes a path to God.

Dante's *Convivio* III 8 discusses beauty in ways that echo earlier sources and anticipate Marinella's account. First, the soul manifests itself as beauty in the face of a woman.[162] Second, the beauty of a woman is compared to the sun and to "small flames of fire"; both of these images involve the association of beauty with light.[163] For Dante, then, beauty is the quality of the soul made manifest in light, and a sign that an essential form has been perfectly realized. For Marinella, because beauty is the perfect realization of a species form it is also a sign of the metaphysical perfection of women.

The most influential of Marinella's near-contemporary sources for the argument from beauty was Ficino's ontology in the *de Amore* (his commentary on Plato's *Symposium*), a Christianized interpretation of Plato's dialogue strongly influenced by Plotinus. Ficino identifies God as the Good itself, who "created first the Angelic Mind, then the Soul of this World as Plato would have it, and last, the Body of the World"; this corresponds roughly to Plotinus's principles (the One, Intellect, Soul, and Matter).[164] One point that Marinella adapted from Ficino and Dante was the assertion that beauty is not fundamentally bodily in nature; this is the significance of describing beauty as a kind of light. Ficino makes much of the imagery of light, which he takes to be incorporeal, claiming that "the principle itself of beauty cannot be body" since the virtues, which are incorporeal, are beautiful and hence those who "thirst after beauty ... must seek [it] elsewhere than in the river of matter."[165] To make the point, Marinella quotes another contemporary Platonist, Leone Ebreo, in the *Essortationi*, who "says that beauty is a ray, a light from the supreme good, which emanates from a well-shaped body and shows us how to rise to heaven to contemplate the origin and cause of perfect beauty."[166] This is the philosophical background that warrants Marinella's claim that beauty is a kind of grace, or ray of light, that is essentially incorporeal, divine in its ultimate origin, and such as to inspire a desire to achieve a knowledge of God.

---

[161] St. Augustine, *Enarrationes in psalmos* CXLIV, 13; P.L. 37, 1878.

[162] Dante, *Convivio* III: viii, 10–11.

[163] Dante, *Convivio* III: viii, 14–15. On beauty as a kind of light see J. A. Mazzeo, "The Augustinian Conception of Beauty and Dante's *Convivio*," *The Journal of Aesthetics and Art Criticism*, 15:4 (1957), p. 447.

[164] M. Ficino, *Commentary on Plato's Symposium*, S. R. Jayne (trans. and intro.) (Columbia: University of Missouri, 1944) p. 127.

[165] M. Ficino, *Commentary on Plato's Symposium*, pp. 167–169, 171.

[166] Marinella, *Exhortations*, p. 196.

7.4 Beauty as Epistemological

In a passage quoted in Section 7.2, Marinella is also making a point about women's epistemological superiority to men by linking two philosophical images from different sources. The staircase she refers to is the series of possible objects of human love, beginning with the beauty of an individual body, that Plato mentions at *Symposium* 211 c. The golden chain of Homer came to be identified by Marinella with the staircase (or ladder) of love objects in the *Symposium*, because the links in the chain are also steps in the staircase. Just as links lower in the chain are less worthy than those that are higher, so too any being on a higher step (or link) is closer to the contemplation of God. The golden chain suggests that the connections among the ascending steps in the progress from the love of individual bodies to the love of the Good itself (or God) are causal rather than logical – each link leads upward to the next; Marinella sees these causal links of the chain as importantly different from the "independent" steps of a staircase.[167]

We have seen that the metaphysics of Plotinus offered a systematic ontology, endorsed by Ficino and other Renaissance Platonists, that supported Marinella's use of the metaphors of the golden chain, particularly in tracing all being back to the One (or God, on Christian interpretations). In the ontology proposed by Plotinus the relation of everything with the One is also one of contemplation: "since the supreme realities devote themselves to contemplation, all other beings must aspire to it, too, because the origin of all things is their end as well."[168] That is, because our origin is in God (because he is the efficient cause of our being and bestows on us the formal cause of our being), it is also natural to us to seek to contemplate and thus return to God as our end (or final cause). Marinella relies on this idea that there is a connection between the ontological origins of our being and the desire to come to know that origin; God is both the cause of our being, and, *because* he is that cause, he is also the ultimate object of our desire. We manifest that desire in an epistemological ascent toward God.

The notion of an ascent from lesser to nobler objects of knowledge derives from the speech of Socrates in Plato's *Symposium*, and its interpretation in Ficino, which Marinella clearly references in contrasting the golden chain with a staircase. The *Symposium* unfolds as a series of speeches in praise of love. Socrates makes a number of points that are central to Marinella's discussion of beauty: (i) he identifies the beautiful with the good.[169] That identification is a fundamental point of departure in Marinella's argument from beauty. Socrates also reports the speech of Diotima, in which she establishes: (ii) a distinction

---

[167] L. Shapiro, "The Outward and Inward Beauty of Early Modern Women," *Revue Philosophique de La France et de l'Étranger*, 203:3 (2013), pp. 331–332.
[168] Plotinus, *Enneads*, III.8.7.   [169] Plato, *Symposium*, 201c.

between the lover and beloved, according to which the object of love is beautiful (and, by implication, good) but the lover is not (yet) immortal, beautiful, good, or wise and so pursues those qualities;[170] (iii) since the good is beautiful, love (or erotic desire) is wanting to possess the good forever, and possessing the good forever amounts to "reproduction and birth in beauty."[171] Elaborating on the notion of reproduction, (iv) Diotima draws another distinction, between those who are "pregnant in body" and pursue women in order to produce mortal offspring, and those who are "pregnant in soul," who aim to produce wisdom, moderation, justice, and "every kind of virtue."[172] The former experience "earthly" love, and the latter "heavenly" love. (v) These latter, who seem to be men, ascend a series of metaphorical steps – a kind of staircase of love – in which they move from the love of beautiful bodies to the ultimate object of love, the Good itself,[173] "starting out from beautiful things and using them like rising stairs."[174]

In the *Nobiltà* Marinella makes use of each of these points, but redraws the role of women. Women are good because they are beautiful; they are beloved by men because they are better than men; in order to produce virtuous actions, men seek out women for "reproduction and birth in beauty"; but women are already closer to God than men, and have a shorter ascent to arrive at knowledge of, and union with, God. Marinella uses the argument from beauty, then, not only to establish the metaphysical superiority of women over men, but also to establish the intellectual possibilities of women, in particular their capacity to achieve a knowledge of God more easily than men.[175]

7.5 Beauty as Moral

The first part of Marinella's argument from beauty is intended then to establish the metaphysical and epistemological superiority of women. The second part makes the case that it is men, not women, who suffer from unchaste desire and that men are thus morally – and not just metaphysically and epistemologically – worse than women. Marinella takes as a matter of fact that there is an asymmetry between erotic desire as experienced by men and by women, which is to be explained by the position of men relative to women in the golden chain. She claims that men desire women, while women do not desire men – or, if they

---

[170] Plato, *Symp.* 203e-204c.

[171] Plato, *Symp.* 206a, 206e-207a. This idea circulated widely in the Renaissance, for example, in the influential dialogue *Gli Asolani* by Pietro Bembo (II, VI XVII), and in Castiglione's *Il Cortegiano* (IV, 51). It appears in pro-woman works, such as Capra's *Della eccellenza e dignità delle donne* (p. 97).

[172] Plato, *Symp.* 208e-209e.   [173] Plato, *Symp.* 210a-211a.   [174] Plato, *Symp.* 211c.

[175] Firenzuolo had already suggested that women might climb the ladder of love, as did Leone Ebreo; see L. Panizza, "Platonic Love on the Rocks: Castiglione Counter-Currents in Renaissance Italy" in *Laus Platonici Philosophi* (Leiden: Brill, 2011), pp. 208, 210.

seem to, it is because they are assuming a polite pretence as a kindness to their admirers. That claim must be understood in the context of the golden chain: because women as a sex constitute a prior link on the chain, they are nearer to the divine than are men. Since desire is always ultimately for the divine, women have no reason to desire men, who are posterior to and lower than them on the chain. Women are more loveable, and more desirable, than men, precisely because they are in closer proximity to the divine. Men have nothing that women do not have, and thus nothing that women might wish to possess, and so women have no reason to desire men. This argument was important for Marinella in allowing her to counter misogynist accusations that women suffer from excessive, lascivious desire, leading men astray from the path of virtue. That is, her claims about beauty and desire were intended to establish the superior moral virtue of women with respect to sexual continence.

The metaphysical and epistemological claims of the beauty argument – that women are nearer in the series of created beings to God, that women therefore have easier access to knowledge of God, and that men can ascend to a knowledge of God only by first recognizing the beauty and virtue of women – have moral implications that are implicit in the account of the *Symposium* and its interpretation in later Christian authors. When God is identified with the Form of the Good, and when the ultimate aim of erotic experience is to acquire knowledge of the Good, erotic experience becomes a route to moral knowledge. Marinella's literary and philosophical predecessors emphasized these moral implications. They altered, however, the Platonic account, in which men are the primary objects of desire for those with "heavenly" love and women the objects of desire for "earthly" love; in most Renaissance interpretations homoerotic love is ignored or disparaged, and the assumption is that the object of both heavenly and earthly love will be a woman.

Dante's *Convivio* identifies the beautiful with the good, and suggests that men can be morally improved through the contemplation of the beauty of women.[176] This is a Christian interpretation of the idea in Plato's *Symposium* that there is moral value to be found in physical beauty insofar as it prompts us to move toward the Form of the Good, identified by Dante with God and our own beatitude.[177] On this view, men desire women because they recognize in the beauty of women the goodness that they themselves lack, and wish to possess. Ficino, like Plato, distinguished "earthly" from "heavenly" erotic desire. For him, "heavenly" desire corresponds to the impulse to contemplate, or "the ability of the soul to know divinity."[178] This is the capacity to be led from

---

[176] Dante, *Convivio*, III: viii, 20–21.   [177] Dante, *Convivio* III: viii, 4–5.
[178] Ficino, *Commentary on Plato's Symposium*, p. 191.

physical beauty upward toward knowledge of God, which implies that men depend upon women to initiate their progression toward God and virtue.

In Plato's *Symposium* it is men who are the objects of the erotic desire characterized as "heavenly." The Christian interpretations that were widespread when Marinella was writing were significantly different in assuming that the objects of men's erotic desire were primarily women, and Marinella exploits that assumption. For example, Agnolo Fierenzuola, in *On the Beauty of Women*, writes: "a beautiful woman is the most beautiful object one can admire, and beauty is the greatest gift God bestowed on His human creatures. And so, through her virtue we direct our souls to contemplation, and through contemplation to the desire for heavenly things."[179] The notion that beauty is incorporeal and divine provided an antecedent for Marinella's distinction between mere physical beauty and the beauty that is a ray of light from the soul and ultimately from God. She reinforced the identification of the beautiful with women, the understanding of the beauty of women as a manifestation of the divine source of their being, and the legitimacy and moral value of desire for women in asserting that women are beautiful, and men are not, that men desire women, but women do not desire men, and that beauty is not, fundamentally, bodily, but rather a bodily sign that the soul is good.

7.6 Marinella's Adaptations and Innovations

The Platonic traditions that provide the philosophical context for Marinella's argument from beauty generally assume that the *agent* of erotic desire is a man, and imply that men are nobler than women insofar as they construe "earthly" love as eroticism directed at women and the reproduction of offspring. In the ancient context, the assumption is often also that the *object* of earthly desire will be a woman, while the object of "heavenly" desire will be a man. In the Renaissance, however, the object of both earthly and heavenly love is assumed to be a woman, and that assumption affords an opportunity to Marinella to adapt and revise certain ideas that have their origin in the ancient world.

First, Platonist authors usually assert that the good is beautiful, but not necessarily that the beautiful is good. Marinella, however, often conflates moral and aesthetic value in the *Nobiltà* (as we have seen in Section 4.3), which allows her to assume that anything that is beautiful will also be good; for her, beauty entails goodness. Relying on the received view of contemporary poets that women are more beautiful than men, she could then claim that it follows that women are more virtuous than men.

Second, Marinella developed an account of the beauty of women as spiritual rather than physical, by relying on the metaphor of beauty as a ray of light

---

[179] A. Firenzuola, *On the Beauty of Women*, K. Eisenbichler and J. Murray (trans. and eds.) (Philadelphia: University of Pennsylvania Press, 1992), p. 11.

emanating from the soul, with its ultimate source in God. The Platonist ontology of emanation allowed her to elaborate the idea that the beauty of the body is not so much an arrangement of parts or features as a spiritual light that signals the beauty of the soul. Because a beautiful soul will be a soul that is a perfect realization of the species form, Marinella is then able to argue that the beauty of women is a manifestation of the perfection of their form, and hence of their superiority to men.

Third, in the *Symposium* and its Renaissance interpretations it is the lover, rather than the beloved, who is of interest. That is, the person who experiences erotic desire for another is the one who may ascend the staircase toward the Good Itself; the object of erotic desire is merely a stepping stone. The lover is an intellectual and moral agent, capable of epistemic progress and moral achievement, while the beloved does not have these capacities. A remarkable feature of Marinella's discussion of beauty is that she turns our attention away from the experience and possibilities of the lover of beautiful bodies, who is a man on every account, including her own, and toward the experience and possibilities of the beloved, who possesses the beautiful body and is, on her account, a woman. She projects some of the status of God onto women, insofar as she bestows a kind of agency on women that parallels that of the divine in Aristotelian metaphysics, in which God acts on other things not by moving himself but by acting as an object of desire, a final cause, for other things.[180] On her account then, women are not passive objects of male desire but rather agents whose beauty *acts* to draw men toward them, and to lead men upward to a knowledge of God himself.

Finally, Marinella was skillful in exploiting the tension between the philosophical idea that only men are worthy of love or are properly beautiful, and the Christian prohibition on homoerotic relationships. Christian interpretations of the "staircase of love" faced some difficulty in accommodating the idea that the first step on the staircase was an individual beautiful body, because norms of Christian morality excluded the possibility that there might be moral benefit in sexual desire, except in strictly codified circumstances.[181] This was complicated by the assumption in Plato's *Symposium* that both lover and beloved would be men. Ficino in *De amore* seems both to accept that homosociality might lead to erotic desire, and also to disapprove of such desire.[182] In asserting

---

[180] Aristotle, *Metaphysics* XII.7 1072b1-13.

[181] For a discussion of the difficulty of reconciling physical desire with Christian norms, see K. Crawford, "Marsilio Ficino, Neoplatonism, and the Problem of Sex," *Renaissance and Reformation*, 28:2 (2004), pp. 3–35.

[182] M. Ficino, *Commentaire sur le banquet de Platon*, R. Marcel (ed. and trans.) (Paris: Les belles lettres, 1956), pp. 251, 253; see also M. Ficino, *Commentary on Plato's Symposium*, p. 208 and note.

that woman are the objects of men's sexual desire, but not themselves subject to desire for men, Marinella was manipulating an ideal of Christian womanhood to make a philosophical point: that the desire men experience for women is proof of the superiority of women over men – metaphysical and epistemological superiority with respect to proximity to the divine, and moral superiority in being impervious to the desires of the flesh.

7.7 Beauty between the *Nobiltà* and the *Essortationi*

As we have seen, Marinella is unequivocal in the *Nobiltà* that beauty is spiritual, that it is a sign of the moral superiority of women to which men are drawn, and that it can help men to improve both intellectually and morally by leading them to a knowledge of God. Marinella's views on beauty in the *Essortationi* appear to be quite different. In this subsection I consider whether it should be read as a rejection of the views on beauty that Marinella had expressed in the *Nobiltà*.

In the *Nobiltà* Marinella suggests that the beauty of women is a feature of every member of the sex, while allowing for differences in the degree of beauty. She concludes her discussion of beauty saying "that women, being more beautiful than men, are also nobler than they are."[183] This is clearly a claim about women as a sex, but Marinella does not preclude exceptions and variations. She says that "the Idea of a charming woman adorned with beauty is nobler than that of a less beautiful and pleasing one, because Ideas exist of particular people";[184] this is clearly an acknowledgement that some women are more beautiful than others, with the implication that some women will be more virtuous than others, if beauty is a sign of virtue. Moreover, in an effort to support her claim that the beauty of the body is primarily spiritual rather than physical, she says: "if it [corporeal beauty] came solely from the body, each body would be beautiful, which it is not."[185] In this context, her point may be just that the bodies of women are more beautiful than the bodies of men, but it seems to leave open the possibility that there are variations in the beauty of women. Considering the question from another angle, Marinella allows for variations in virtue among women, which seems to imply variations in beauty. She says: "There have been some men who, on discovering a woman who was not very good, have bitingly and slanderously stated that all women are bad and wicked."[186] So there are some women, on Marinella's account, who are "not very good"; nonetheless, she asserts that "among women the virtuous far outnumber the bad."[187] She believes, then, that some women will be less

---

[183] Marinella, *Nobility*, p. 68.   [184] Marinella, *Nobility*, p. 53.   [185] Marinella, *Nobility*, p. 59.
[186] Marinella, *Nobility*, p. 121.   [187] Marinella, *Nobility*, p. 124.

virtuous than others, and hence less beautiful, but also insists that women as a sex are more virtuous and more beautiful than men.

The basis for this claim of universal beauty in the *Nobiltà* depends on two features of her argument. First, because she claims in the *Nobiltà* that beauty is not properly physical, but rather psychological or spiritual, it is not a claim that every woman has perfectly proportioned features or any other objective feature. Second, because it emerges from the idea that women are innately superior to men, as constituting a higher link on the golden chain that represents the series of created beings, it is in fact a claim about moral rather than physical superiority. So, in the *Nobiltà* to say that women are more beautiful than men is (a) a general claim about women as a kind that allows for exceptions and (b) a claim about a moral rather than a physical state.

In the *Essortationi* Marinella's views on beauty are significantly different in two respects. The less important respect concerns cosmetics and other aids to beauty. Marinella defends the use of cosmetics in the *Nobiltà* (perhaps reflecting her father's views and interests).[188] She draws no distinction between natural and artificial beauty, and does not disapprove of artificial means to enhance or preserve the beauty of the body. In general, she is uncritical of women who might employ cosmetics. In the *Essortationi*, however, she clearly disapproves of cosmetic improvements and refers to women's dependence on them as "servitude."[189]

The more important difference concerns a central claim in the *Nobiltà*, that beauty is primarily spiritual. Marinella makes conflicting claims on this point in the *Essortationi*. Having said that "it is impossible to deny that beauty is . . . an image of or a ray that derives from divine beauty," she goes on to say:

> Beauty is not a celestial light, but an earthly and mortal one. Were it divine, as many philosophers maintain and as I myself stated in my chapter on beauty in *The Nobility and Excellence of Women*, I do not believe it would flee and vanish as quickly as it does.[190]

How should we interpret these inconsistent claims – that "no one can deny" that beauty is a ray of light from the divine, and that "[b]eauty is not a celestial light" – which occur within the same discussion? Some commentators see Marinella offering here, in explicit terms, a retraction of the position she adopted in the *Nobiltà*.[191] That is, one interpretation is that we witness with this claim, and with the *Essortationi* more generally, Marinella changing her

---

[188] Marinella, *Nobility*, pp. 166–167.   [189] Marinella, *Exhortations*, pp. 112–113.
[190] Marinella, *Exhortations*, pp. 196–197.
[191] See Benedetti, "Introduction" in Marinella, *Exhortations*; see also L. Benedetti, "Arcangela Tarabotti e Lucrezia Marinella: appunti per un dialogo mancato," *Modern Language Notes* 129:3S (2014), pp. 87–97.

mind, and rejecting the idea that beauty is primarily spiritual. But in that case it is odd that she begins with the claim that beauty is a divine light.

This apparent retraction seems to rely on an equivocation between divine and merely human beauty. In the *Nobiltà*'s discussion of beauty, it is clear that Marinella conceives of it in nonphysical terms, such that the beauty of the body is just a kind of light from the soul. The beauty that "flees and vanishes" in this passage from the *Essortationi* cannot be the spiritual beauty derived ultimately from the divine. It must rather be, as Marinella writes, "the vague quality" that is produced by "the combination and arrangement of colors."[192] Beauty as this "human splendor" is distinct, in the *Essortationi*, from the notion of beauty as a "divine light." If this is right, we can understand the apparently conflicting claims as consistent. The beauty that is an image of divine beauty and derives from it, is the "divine light." But this divine light may not be evident to all; Marinella's suggestion seems to be that there is another beauty, an "earthly and mortal light" that derives not from God but from "the harmony of well-disposed parts."[193]

This mortal light is the focus of the sexual desire experienced by men for women. We can see this when Marinella allows in the *Essortationi* that beauty that is earthly and mortal, mere human splendor, "fades" – namely alters over time. It is significant that when beauty does fade, moral virtue can compensate for its absence, which is to say that the beauty that is an emanation of light from the soul is preserved in virtue. This is consistent with the golden chain passage in the *Nobiltà*, and it suggests a way in which what appear to be two different conceptions of beauty can cohere. If moral virtue can "compensate" for physical beauty that has faded, it is because moral virtue is itself a kind of beauty – and perhaps, indeed, a "truer," in the sense of metaphysically prior, kind of beauty.[194]

Marinella's concern about cosmetic use in the *Essortationi* indicates a new distinction, and a new set of considerations. She differentiates "natural" and "artificial" beauty, approving of the former and disapproving of the latter. This implies that, while she continues to hold the view that natural, spiritual beauty is fundamental, and that it is an emanation of the divine, and prior to any artifice, she no longer believes that there is no moral danger in the enhancement of this natural beauty through artificial means. What exactly is that danger? Marinella's emphasis in the *Essortationi* is on how fickle the love of men is for women of fading beauty: "Therefore, my beloved women, do not put faith in something fleeting that clears the path more quickly than does a leopard or a hare"; "the

---

[192] Marinella, *Exhortations*, p. 198.   [193] Marinella, *Exhortations*, p. 197.
[194] Marinella, *Exhortations,* pp. 201–202.

beauty that was once compared to that of an angel turns into the ugliness of a demon from hell ... therefore, you must try to overcome these natural defects and flaws through virtue."[195] The danger is that by shoring up natural beauty with cosmetics one might be pandering to the superficial desire of men rather than focusing on the virtue of one's own soul, a possession for all time.[196]

8 Virtue

8.1 Introduction

The virtues of women and the vices of men are two of the central themes of the *Nobiltà*. The title of the polemic itself suggests the importance of the concept of virtue for Marinella; as we saw in Section 4.2, the term "*nobiltà*" refers to an innate capacity to develop virtue, and "*eccellenze*" to the virtues that develop from *nobiltà* under the right conditions. We have already seen that Marinella's argument for the superiority of women is founded on the greater capacity for virtue that makes their souls superior to those of men. But her claim is not only that women have a greater capacity, but that they *realize* that capacity by acquiring the dispositions that are virtues and manifesting those dispositions in their actions. The virtues women display are one kind of evidence that Marinella adduces in asserting that women are superior to men. As we saw in Section 7, when she introduces the idea that the beauty of women is a sign of the superiority of their souls, she also refers to another kind of evidence: the "effects" (*gli effetti*) of their souls.[197] These "effects," I suggest, are the virtues that Marinella claims women have to a greater degree than men: the dispositions and actions of a woman are direct manifestations of the virtues that make women's souls better.

Before reviewing Marinella's argument that women are – or would be, under the right conditions – more virtuous than men, and what implications she draws from that claim in the *Nobiltà* and the *Essortationi*, consider Marinella's conception of virtue, which is derived from Aristotelian as well as Christian sources. The influence of Aristotle is notable in both the *Nobiltà* and the *Essortationi*, in that Marinella often introduces her discussion of a virtue by referring to Aristotle's definition. A virtue, in this tradition, may be either intellectual or moral: an intellectual virtue is a disposition to grasp the truth, whether theoretical or practical, and a moral virtue is a disposition to act according to right reason (see Section 5.2 for the division of the soul that warrants this distinction).[198] On Aristotle's account, while there are many intellectual virtues, one in particular is necessary for the acquisition of moral

---

[195] Marinella, *Exhortations*, pp. 200–201.   [196] Marinella, *Exhortations*, p. 203.
[197] Marinella, *Nobility*, p. 55.   [198] Aristotle, *EN* I.13 1103a4-7.

virtue: *phronêsis*, a virtue belonging to practical reason. It is the ability to determine which action available to an agent will be in accordance with right reason, together with the desire to perform that action; Aristotle says it is a "reasoned and true state of capacity to act with regard to human goods."[199]

Every moral virtue is thus a disposition to act according to right reason, but they vary according to the context in which they are required. For example, the virtue of temperance will be a disposition to feel and to act for the sake of the good with respect to pleasure and pain; the virtue of courage will be a disposition to act for the sake of the good in the face of death. In general, practical wisdom is associated with correct judgment (knowing what is good), and moral virtues with correct desire (wanting to do what is good). Knowledge and desire are mutually necessary, on Aristotle's account, because we cannot desire what is good unless we know what is good, and we cannot act on that knowledge unless we have the correct desires. Thus both the intellectual and the moral virtues are necessary if we are to lead good lives, either as individuals or as communities – Marinella, like Aristotle, treats the moral life of a person as one that is embedded in a political community.

The development and manifestation of human virtue depends on the innate capacity for virtue. This capacity is, on Marinella's account, the nobility intrinsic to every person, but it must be cultivated through education and through the practice of virtuous actions (the process that Aristotle calls "habituation"). In other words, nobility is a necessary but not a sufficient condition for the acquisition of human virtue. Once a person has been educated and has been habituated to virtuous actions, they will acquire the virtues, which, again, are settled dispositions, intellectual and moral. But virtue requires action: the virtuous person must enact their virtues and not simply be disposed to act in certain ways, so that opportunities to act virtuously must be afforded to a person if they are to be fully virtuous. This is the theory of virtue that Marinella relies on in developing her argument for the virtue of women.

8.2 Women and Virtue

In Part One of the *Nobiltà*, in the chapter entitled "Of the nature and essence of the female sex," Marinella argues, as we have seen, that women are nobler than men, which is to say that they have a greater innate capacity for virtue than men do. She goes farther in the subsequent chapter, "Of women's noble actions and virtues, which greatly surpass men's, as will be proved by reasoning and example," arguing not only that women have a greater capacity, but also that they are able to *realize* that capacity to develop the dispositions that are the

---

[199] Aristotle, *EN* VI.5 1140b20-21.

virtues, and that when they do, those dispositions are better – more stable, stronger – than men's, and are manifested in actions that surpass men's in their virtue. The "nature and essence of the female sex" is this capacity for virtue, and the "noble actions and virtues" are the acts and the dispositions to act that constitute the virtues in practice. Marinella's argument is then that women are better both with respect to capacity and in the fulfillment of that capacity.

Marinella's argument proceeds from the assumption that in a human being both the soul and the body are "principles" on which the "operations" or actions of a person depend.[200] As we have seen in Sections 5 and 6, she claims that with respect to each of these principles women are superior to men; their souls are nobler (i.e. are more naturally suited to the development of human virtues), and their bodies more temperate and therefore better adapted to act as instruments of the soul. The body of a woman is thus "a fitting shelter for kindness and virtue."[201] Bodies, like souls, can be "excellent." Although the excellences of a body will be different from those of a soul, a bodily excellence such as a moderate temperature has value precisely because it supports the realization of intellectual and moral virtues.

In discussing the virtues of women, Marinella emphasizes two kinds. One kind includes temperance and its subdivisions, gentleness, sobriety, and chastity. We have seen how important it is to Marinella to demonstrate that, despite popular misogynist stereotypes, women exhibit more self-control than men with respect to their appetites and desires, which is what it means to say that they have the virtue of temperance. That capacity for self-control is important, as we will see in Section 9, not only to the life of the individual, but also in the political context, and Marinella foregrounds temperance not only because it is a crucial aspect of the character of the virtuous individual but also because it is especially significant for anyone with political power.

The second kind of virtue that she emphasizes in the *Nobiltà* is precisely a set of political excellences. Marinella focuses on two virtues that might not immediately appear to be such: proficiency in the sciences and in "the military arts."[202] By "the sciences" Marinella means any body of learning (including "letters").[203] It is striking that these are virtues usually understood as masculine, and so in dwelling on them Marinella is asserting that women have a natural entitlement to domains of activity that were usually reserved for men. The first, a command of a domain of learning, is plainly an intellectual virtue; the second seems to combine both intellectual and moral virtues, since it involves certain kinds of knowledge (e.g., of strategy and tactics), but also certain moral states:

---

[200] Marinella, *Nobility*, p. 77.   [201] Marinella, *Nobility*, p. 78.   [202] Marinella, *Nobility*, p. 78.
[203] Marinella, *Nobility*, p. 79.

courage, in particular (Marinella cites Ariosto speaking of "valiant women" and Plato referring to those women who have "valor").[204] It is clear that Marinella introduces the virtues of knowledge of the sciences and of the military arts here in order to conclude that women "would govern empires better than men," that is, to insist on the political value of the virtues of which she argues women are capable.[205] Women, Marinella says, would govern better because they have (or might have, if educated and habituated) "greater practical wisdom, justice, and experience of life."[206] Practical wisdom, as we have seen in Sections 5.2 and 8.1, is the capacity to deliberate and identify the correct course of action, the primary skill both of the virtuous person and of the virtuous ruler, and justice is a crucial virtue in those who govern.

Marinella anticipates the objection that most women are not in fact learned or skilled in the military arts. That, she asserts, is not because they are incapable of acquiring such virtues but rather because "men, fearing to lose their authority and become women's servants, often forbid them even to learn to read or write."[207] Since virtues require instruction, cultivation, and habituation through practice, a person who is given no instruction, and prevented from cultivating or practicing the virtues, will not acquire them.

> If [women] do not show their skills, it is because men do not allow them to practice them, since they are driven by obstinate ignorance, which persuades them that women are not capable of learning the things they do. I would like these men to try the experiment of training a good-natured boy and girl of about the same age and intelligence in letters and arms. They would see how much sooner the girl would become expert than the boy and how she would surpass him completely.[208]

In this passage Marinella is clearly referring to the distinction between the capacity for virtue, the realization of that capacity as a disposition through practice or habituation, and its manifestation in action. She assumes still that girls will be more naturally adept at learning ("she would surpass him completely"), and acknowledges that that natural capacity must be cultivated to realize itself as a disposition that will govern action.

From this discussion we can see that Marinella makes four different points about women and virtue in the *Nobiltà*. The first is that women are capable of greater virtue (both intellectual and moral) than men because their souls are bestowed with greater nobility, the capacity to develop human virtue, and because their bodies are more temperate. The second is that the virtues of which women are more capable include those that are usually treated as the

---

[204] Marinella, *Nobility*, pp. 78–79. [205] Marinella, *Nobility*, p. 79.
[206] Marinella, *Nobility*, p. 79. [207] Marinella, *Nobility*, p. 79. [208] Marinella, *Nobility*, p. 80.

province of men; Marinella effectively dismantles the idea that certain virtues are available or appropriate only to one sex. The third point is that the reason that many women, despite their greater capacity for virtue, do not actually develop greater virtue, is that they are deprived of education and the opportunities to become habituated in any virtue except those traditionally viewed as feminine. So women both have a greater *capacity* for virtue, and, when that capacity is cultivated, greater *developed* virtue, including purportedly masculine virtues. The fourth is that women are better suited to political rule precisely because they have a greater capacity than men for virtue and develop greater virtue than men unless they are prevented from doing so.

8.3 Vice and Men

Part Two of the *Nobiltà* paints a portrait of the moral character of men that contrasts in every respect with that of women, and so acts as a reverse-portrait of the character of women. It is a discussion of the many vices to which Marinella maintains men are peculiarly liable, and is intended to support her argument in the first part: that women are nobler than men and more virtuous. It is striking that she accuses men of many of the vices that Passi had attributed to women in his *I donneschi difetti*: pride, avarice, envy, ambition, ingratitude, cruelty, vanity. She includes chapters on some of the primary ancient vices (corresponding to the cardinal virtues of Christianity), each of which has a corresponding virtue that she has claimed women exhibit: intemperance/temperance (ch. 3); injustice/justice (ch. 10); cowardice/courage (ch. 17), as well as many chapters on what might seem to be minor vices (self-embellishment [ch. 22] and chattiness [ch. 14]). She also accuses men of particular Christian vices: heresy (ch. 23), disrespect of God (ch. 18), and particular sins (e.g., murder [ch. 30 and 31]). What emerges is a portrait of men as base and wicked in every sense, contrasted with an implied portrait of women as temperate, just, courageous, and practically wise.

Marinella carefully accuses men of those vices most often attributed to women in the misogynistic literature: volubility (ch. 14 and 27), cowardice (ch. 17 and 24), laziness (ch. 7), inconstancy (ch. 14 and 11), untruthfulness (ch. 20), vanity (ch. 22), and silliness (ch. 29). The importance of this is not only to darken the picture of men's vices, but to defend women against the charge that they are morally weak and intellectually feeble. It is striking, too, that Marinella opens her discussion of men's vices with a series of individual vices (avarice, envy, intemperance, anger, pride, laziness) that collectively emphasize the lack of control men seem to have over their appetites for money, pleasure, or accomplishment. The effect of this is to emphasize that men do not have their desires in the keeping of their reason. That, of course, is the point Marinella has made in the argument from physiology (see Section 6): because men are hotter, their appetites and desires are excessive and mistaken in ways that interfere with the operation of reason. It is thus men, not women, on Marinella's account, who are morally weak in ways that interfere with their exercise of reason. Implicit in the reversal of the gendered associations with these particular vices is Marinella's claim that women are capable of even those virtues that are usually associated with men.

Marinella makes a point of including in Part Two chapters on certain vices with particular political resonance: men are tyrannical, seditious, unjust, and prone to the pursuit of glory over the pursuit of the good. This is especially significant in light of her contention in Part One of the *Nobiltà* that women are more virtuous than men in ways that make them better suited to ruling over others. Marinella's point is that the vices of men make them especially unfit for political rule and especially dangerous when they do achieve political power. So this enumeration of the vices of men supports not only the claim that women are nobler than men, but more specifically the claim that it is women, rather than men, who should exercise political rule.

8.4 Virtue in the *Nobiltà* and the *Essortationi*

At a first glance, Marinella's views on women and virtue change radically in the years between the publication of the *Nobiltà* and that of the *Essortationi*: in the latter she seems to argue for a traditional role for women, secluded in the home, devoted to the domestic arts, focused on family, and evaluated according to the virtues traditionally deemed appropriate for women: chastity, restraint in speech, submission to husbands. This appearance is, however, deceptive. There is considerable evidence that the *Essortationi* is not so much advocating women's submission as testifying to the many ways in which the capacities of women are neglected, thwarted, and abused.[209] Certainly, in each exhortation Marinella systematically undermines or qualifies her initial claims in ways that suggest that women are in fact superior to men, as in the *Nobiltà*. For example, in the first exhortation, advocating the seclusion of women, she begins by citing Gorgias as saying that "a woman's reputation must not leave the walls of her home."[210] But two points tell against reading this as her settled view. First, Marinella almost certainly took as her source for this a passage in Plutarch's *Mulierum Virtutes*, and Gorgias according to Plutarch in fact *disagrees* with Thucydides' who, according to Plutarch, believed that "the name of the good woman, like her person, ought to be shut up indoors and never go out."[211] So the

---

[209] See n. 34 and n. 35.   [210] Marinella, *Exhortations*, p. 43.

[211] Plutarch, *Moralia*, 242e-f, Frank Cole Babbitt (trans.) (Cambridge, MA: Harvard University Press, 1968), 3.475; see also Sinclair, "Latin," pp. 122–123.

ancient source she cites in support of the seclusion of women in fact does not agree that a woman should not have a public reputation. Second, the reason that Marinella offers for advocating the seclusion of women is that "excellent things should not be exposed to people's desire or judgment" and since "God and nature have assigned such seclusion to women," that suggests that the great dignity of women is the reason why they should be secluded, like God himself and our souls, which are "secluded" in our bodies – not visible to the senses.[212]

In another example, in the second exhortation against the study of literature, Marinella's argument is not that women are incapable of study, but rather that their efforts will be neglected, patronised, or derided, or men will cast doubt on the authorship of women.[213] In a third example, the seventh exhortation, on practical wisdom or prudence, urges women to choose a husband carefully since they will be expected to follow his model; Marinella traces any vice in women to the model provided by their husbands, and asserts that a woman whose husband is vicious should not follow his example or be subject to his authority.[214] As in the case of beauty, so too in the case of virtue, the differences between the *Nobiltà* and the *Essortationi* are less significant than they may at first appear. In each case, an admonition to adopt conventional norms is justified not by the nature of women, but rather by the consequences for women of the viciousness of men.

9 Tyranny and Liberty

9.1 Context in the Sixteenth Century

Marinella was writing in a philosophical context in which moral and political claims were often interlinked. As a consequence, her conception of the virtues, and her claim that women are more virtuous than men – both in the sense that they have a greater capacity for virtue and in the sense that when that capacity is cultivated the result is more consistent and perfected virtues – had political implications. In particular, the question of virtue was connected to the question of the innate liberty of human beings, and how political life should be structured in recognition of that. The idea was this: because human beings, unlike non-human animals, have a free will, bestowed on them by God, they are responsible moral agents capable both of sin and of virtue. If, then, we deny that women have the liberty of action implied by possession of a free will, we are denying them moral agency. If we deny them agency, however, we cannot hold them morally responsible for their actions, or evaluate their actions in moral

---

[212] Marinella, *Exhortations*, p. 45.   [213] Marinella, *Exhortations*, pp. 56–57.
[214] Marinella, *Exhortations*, pp. 129, 141.

terms. So Marinella, like many pro-woman authors, argued that women did have a free will.

Earlier pro-woman authors had asserted the liberty of women, and deplored the tyranny of men, in terms that Marinella employs. Among the earliest was Mario Equicola, who wrote:

> Since, indeed, the nature of rational mortals is one, liberty is equally innate in all . . . [C]ontrary to divine right and the laws of nature, violent rule, authoritarian regimes, and tyranny are practised; and thus for women that natural liberty either has been prohibited by laws or has ceased to exist through custom.[215]

The basis of Equicola's claim that women are as entitled as men to liberty is the assertion of the identity of the nature of rational mortals; women and men do not constitute different kinds. Henricus Cornelius Agrippa also attributed natural liberty to women, claimed that the source of that liberty was God as well as nature, and construed the power of men as tyrannical, saying "since the excessive tyranny of men prevails over divine right and natural laws, the freedom that was once accorded to women is in our day obstructed by unjust laws, suppressed by custom and usage, reduced to nothing by education."[216] Agrippa, like Equicola, acknowledges that women do not enjoy the liberty that men do, and explains the subjection of women as the result of arbitrary laws, conventions, and education (or its lack). It is thus not a natural state of affairs. The characterization of masculine authority as tyrannical in the works of Equicola and Agrippa is suggestive, but neither provides an analysis of the notions of liberty and tyranny to support these claims.[217]

Marinella provides that analysis, against the background of the development of political theory that was critical of tyranny (particularly in its contrast with republicanism) in sixteenth-century Italian city-states. Among the most influential works were Machiavelli's *Discorsi* (*Discourses*) and, for pro-woman authors, Castiglione's *Il Cortegiano* (*The Courtier*).[218] These accounts of tyranny anticipate some of the central claims made by Marinella. First, in Machiavelli's *Discourses*, we find tyranny associated with inequality, and republican government (as in Marinella's Venice) with equality.[219] Second, both Machiavelli and Castiglione take Aristotle's division of the forms of

---

[215] I am grateful to Stephen Kolsky for his translation of Equicola; this is a modified version.

[216] Agrippa, *Declamation*, p. 94.

[217] See V. Cox, "The Single Self: Feminist Thought and the Marriage Market in Early Modern Venice," *Renaissance Quarterly*, XLVIII (1995), 516–521, for a discussion of earlier defenses of women in which male tyranny figured.

[218] Baldassare Castiglione's *Libro del cortegiano* was first published in Venice in 1528. Niccolò Machiavelli's *Discorsi sopra la prima deca di Tito Livio* was published posthumously in Florence in 1531, but his works were on the Index of Prohibited Books from 1559, and so it is unlikely that the authors I discuss here had easy access to them.

[219] Machiavelli, *Discorsi sopra la prima deca di Tito Livio* (*Discourses*), p. 257.

government in the *Politics* as authoritative, and hence take tyranny to be a mistaken form of rule.[220] Third, both attribute an "evil will," vicious and excessive desires, or self-interest to the tyrant.[221] Finally, both characterize the tyrant as acting with disregard for the law.[222]

In arguing that women, like men, possess an innate liberty that makes their subjection to men unjust, Marinella draws on republican ideology as it was systematized in sixteenth-century Venice. Republican liberty had two senses in the political theory of the Renaissance: a republic was both (i) independent from other states, free from external control, and (ii) self-governed in the sense that it was ruled by its citizens rather than by a monarch or despot.[223] In the funeral orations and letters of Andrea Navagero, Gasparo Contarini's *De magistratibus et republica Venetorum* (*The Republic of Venice*), and the Florentine Donato Giannotti's *Libro della Repubblica de' Veneziani* (*On the Republic of the Venetians*), Venice was represented as a model of this liberty and successful self-governance.[224] The republic of Venice was characterized as a mixed constitution, combining elements of monarchy, aristocracy and democracy, with aristocracy the dominant element.[225] Implicit in this was the suggestion that the primary political value of the Venetian republic was virtue, since aristocracy awards political offices on the basis of excellence. In arguing for the liberty of women Marinella exploits the idea that it is virtue more than any other quality that entitles one to political participation and rule. As we saw in Section 8, her discussion of virtues and their corresponding vices is often inflected by political considerations, and by her ambition to make known women's capacity for political rule.

The Renaissance conception of republicanism as fundamentally opposed to tyranny had its origins in interpretations of ancient Greek and Roman political philosophy, particularly Aristotle's practical philosophy.[226] Two particular

---

[220] Castiglione, *The Courtier*, p. 221; Machiavelli, *Discourses*, pp. 111–112.
[221] Castiglione, *The Courtier*, pp. 223, 230; Machiavelli, *Discourses*, p. 283.
[222] Castiglione, *The Courtier*, p. 221; Machiavelli, *Discourses*, pp. 142–143.
[223] W. J. Bouwsma, *Venice and the Defense of Republican Liberty* (Berkeley: University of California Press, 1968) pp. 12–14; F. Gilbert, "The Venetian Constitution in Florentine Political Thought," in N. Rubinstein (ed.), *Florentine Studies: Politics and Society in Renaissance Florence* (London: Faber and Faber, 1968), p. 466.
[224] The orations and letters of Navagero were composed before 1529 and collected in J. A. Vulpius (ed.), *Andreae Naugerii: Opera Omnia* (Padova: Cominus, 1718). Gasparo Contarini's *Magistratibus et republica Venetorum* was written in 1523/4 and collected in *Gasparis Contareni Cardinalis Opera* (Paris: Sebastianum Nivelium, 1571). Donato Giannotti's dialogue, *Repubblica de' Veneziani*, was written in 1525/6, and collected in his *Opere* (Pisa: Niccolò Capurro, 1819).
[225] L. J. Libby, "Venetian History and Political Thought after 1509," *Studies in the Renaissance* 20 (1973), 12–13, 19; Gilbert, "The Venetian Constitution," pp. 469–471.
[226] For the medieval background to Contarini and Giannotti's political philosophy, see F. C. Lane, "At the Roots of Republicanism," *The American Historical Review* 71:2 (1966), pp. 413–414 and N. Rubinstein, "Political Ideas in Sienese Art: The Frescoes by Ambrogio Lorenzetti and

features of the republicanism contemporary to Marinella's Venice, and drawn from ancient sources, were central to her argument for the liberty of women. First, law rather than any individual should hold the ultimate political authority.[227] Second, those who are equals should be ruled on a basis of equality, and not despotically; for Aristotle free women ought to be ruled on a basis of equality (constitutionally), and not despotically.[228] This is true although there are questions about how Aristotle conceived of this equality, and how he might have reconciled it with the view that men ought by nature to rule over women.[229] Marinella rejects the idea that women are subject to men by nature, while embracing Aristotle's claim that the status of a free woman is different from that of a natural slave.

There are, then, at least three points that Marinella draws from contemporary republican theory, and ancient philosophy, in order to argue that women ought to enjoy the liberty that men do, and that if they were to do so, the city would benefit: (i) that virtue is the primary qualification for political participation, (ii) that law, or reason, is the ultimate authority, and (iii) that republican rule is opposed to tyrannical rule insofar as it treats those who are ruled as equals with those who rule. She makes use of all three points to portray the power that men exercised over women in Venice as tyrannical, and to argue for the natural liberty of women.

9.2 The Psychology of Tyranny

Marinella argues, then, that women are innately free, and hence entitled by nature and by God to the freedoms (of movement, person, and education) that men enjoy, and to freedom from the domination of men; she also argues that men, despite possessing the same innate liberty, are disposed to be tyrannical. In making these arguments, Marinella relies on an understanding of the divisions of the soul and of human psychology drawn from Aristotle's *Nicomachean Ethics* at I. 13 (set out in Section 5.2), but also on the tripartite division proposed by Plato and developed in the Platonist tradition, mediated primarily through the translations and commentaries of Ficino.[230] On her understanding the

---

Taddeo di Bartolo in the Palazzo Pubblico," *Journal of the Warburg and Courtauld Institutes* 21:3/4 (1958), 182–189.

[227] Bouwsma, *Venice*, p. 150.   [228] Aristotle, *Politics* I.12 1259a37-b4.

[229] See Aristotle, *Politics* I. 5 1254b13-14. For an overview of the reception of Aristotle and other ancient authors in Renaissance discussions of women's political status, see Maclean, *Renaissance Notion,* pp. 47–67. For an interpretation that attempts to reconcile Aristotle's claims that women ought to be ruled by nature, but not as slaves, see M. Deslauriers, "Political Rule over Women in *Politics* I," in T. Lockwood and T. Samaras (eds.), *Aristotle's* Politics: *A Critical Guide* (Cambridge: Cambridge University Press, 2015), pp. 55–75.

[230] For a discussion of the reception of Aristotle and Plato in the Renaissance, see C. B. Schmitt, *Aristotle and the Renaissance* (Cambridge: Harvard University Press, 1983) and J. Hankins, *Plato in the Italian Renaissance* (Leiden: Brill, 1990).

rational part of the soul comprises speculative (or theoretical) reason, concerned with unchanging objects of thought, on the one hand, and practical reason, concerned with moral and political action, on the other. Both Plato and Aristotle distinguish reason from nonrational faculties; Marinella draws on both accounts.[231] Her discussion assumes that there is a "spirited" part, which is responsible for the desire for honor and the impulse to anger, and an "appetitive" part which gives rise to the desire for physical pleasure.[232] In a well-ordered soul both the appetitive and the spirited parts should be subjected to the control of reason, so that desires for honor or pleasure are aligned always with the rational desire to achieve the good. These divisions of the soul figure, as we will see, in the accounts of tyranny.

In the argument concerned with liberty and tyranny Marinella draws on a discussion of the parts of the soul and their interactions in Plato's *Republic* IX, where Socrates argues that those with excessive desires both for sensation and for honor are tyrannical in temperament. Socrates divides the soul into three parts, somewhat different from Aristotle's faculties, and attributes to each a corresponding pleasure: a rational part that takes pleasure in learning; a spirited part with which one grows angry and takes pleasure in honor, victory, revenge, and anger itself (similar to Aristotle's faculty of desire); and a sensitive or appetitive part, which takes pleasure in food, drink, and sex.[233] On Socrates' account, when the appetitive or the spirited part of the soul satisfies itself, the soul moves away from reason. So the desires we satisfy, whether rational, sensitive, or spirited, situate us relative to reason, distancing us from it to the extent that we gratify sensual or spirited impulses that have not been sanctioned by reason. Distancing ourselves from reason, we distance ourselves from the law. This is why Socrates associates the satisfaction of nonrational desires with the tyrannical temperament:

> And is not that furthest removed from reason which is furthest from law and order? . . . And was it not made plain that the furthest removed are the erotic and tyrannical appetites? . . . Then the tyrant's place, I think, will be fixed at the furthest remove from true and proper pleasure.[234]

---

[231] For Plato's division of the soul, see *Republic* IV 435c-441c; for Aristotle's division, see also *De anima* II 3 414a29-414b19, where he sets out a more technical account than in the EN of the faculties (δυνάμεις) of the soul. For helpful accounts of these divisions, see H. Lorenz, *The Brute Within: Appetitive Desire in Plato and Aristotle* (Oxford: Oxford University Press, 2006) and J. Moss, "Appearances and Calculations: Plato's Division of the Soul," *Oxford Studies in Ancient Philosophy* 34 (2008), pp. 35–68.

[232] In referring to the division of the soul, Marinella does not distinguish between Platonist and Aristotelian accounts, assert their harmony, or point out divergences.

[233] Plato, *Republic* IX 580d.   [234] Plato, *Republic* IX 587a-b.

It is precisely indulgence in the pleasures of the flesh and the pleasures of victory, revenge and anger, that characterize the tyrant. If we bear in mind Aristotle's physiological account of spiritedness as fostered by heat, and Socrates' political account of spiritedness and the appetites, we can see how Marinella was able to move from the view that a hotter physical constitution produces excessive desires both for pleasure (particularly sexual pleasure) and for honor (which disposes one to anger), to the view that excessive desires and the sensuality and irascibility that accompany them will cause one to develop a tyrannical character. Consider now how she traces this connection.

9.3 Marinella's Argument for Liberty

Among the chapters that Marinella added to the 1601 edition of the *Nobiltà* was one entitled "On tyrannical men and those who usurp state power." In this chapter Marinella says that the tyrant is not governed by any law, but seeks only to satisfy his own will.

> Of all the worst men in the world, I believe none are as bad as the tyrant: since he is not governed by any law. As we can read in Aristotle's *Politics* [IV. 10]: whereas other rulers act to ensure that which is honest and just, the tyrant's aim is his own advantage which governs his reason. The law which governs his actions is whatever pleases him, in other words, his will made law . . . To conclude, according to Aristotle, the tyrant's mind is occupied by these three concerns: first, to make his subjects timid and worthless; second, to ensure that there be no trust amongst them; third, to make them so poor as to be unable to attempt anything of any significance.[235]

Her focus here is on the motives of the tyrant, and the relation between his desires ("his will") and the law. Aristotle had classed tyranny among the incorrect constitutions, which he characterized as those constitutions in which the ruler or rulers pursue their own interests, rather than the interests of those over whom they rule. In seeking to satisfy his own avaricious and violent desires, the tyrant places himself above the law, or treats his own desires as though they simply *were* the law. To do this is to confound reason with desire, since the law represents reason. This is the fundamental moral error of the tyrant: he "seeks his own advantage" rather than what is "honest and just."

In describing tyrannical man, Marinella relies notably on Aristotle's account of the tyrant in the *Politics*, which she reports accurately. She draws in particular on two points from that account that distinguish the legitimate monarch from the tyrant. The first is the assertion that tyranny has three political goals:

---

[235] Marinella, *Nobiltà*, p. 128.

> For tyranny aims at three things; one, that the ruled have only modest thoughts (for a small-souled person will not conspire against anyone); second, that they distrust one another (for a tyranny will not be overthrown before some persons are able to trust each other) . . . ; and third, an incapacity for activity, for no one will undertake something on behalf of those who are incapable, so that not even a tyranny will be overthrown where the capacity is lacking.[236]

For Marinella, this suggests that we should not mistake the tyrant for a political innocent. He pursues his own advantage in the sense that he aims to satisfy his own desires without subjecting them to the scrutiny of reason, but he employs astute methods to ensure the compliance of his subjects, undermining their ambitions, their trust in one another, and their very capacity to act in any way opposed to his will. Unlike the legitimate monarch who rules in the interests of those over whom he rules, the tyrant damages his subjects in ruling over them and seeking his own advantage at their expense.

A second point that Marinella draws from Aristotle is that the tyrant asserts his will in this way over people who are his equals or even his superiors. Marinella cites the passage from Aristotle in which he makes this claim:

> Any monarchy must necessarily be a tyranny of this sort if it rules in unchallenged fashion over persons who are all similar or better, and with a view to its own advantage and not that of the ruled.[237]

A king is one who is genuinely superior to those over whom he rules, but the tyrant rules over those who are his equals. The relative virtue of tyrant and people, and the motive of the tyrant to pursue his own interests, are what make tyrannical power illegitimate. So the tyrant is not only a ruler with excessive desires, exercising power in accordance with those desires rather than according to law and in the interests of his subjects, but also someone who acts this way in relation to people who are "similar or better." For Aristotle, this is a way of saying that his subjects are not natural slaves, people deprived of a faculty of deliberative reason. Tyrannical rule would only be permissible over such people (and even then, Aristotle shies away from using the term "tyrannical" to denote legitimate rule). For Marinella, the point is that women are not natural slaves, but bestowed with practical reason; this is what makes them in a fundamental sense the equals of men, and their capacity to make better use of this reason, because they are unhampered by the excessive and mistaken desires that plague men, is the basis of their ultimate superiority. Women are the equals of men in one sense and their superiors in another.

---

[236] Aristotle, *Politics* V.11 1314a15-25.   [237] Aristotle, *Politics* IV.10 1295a19-22.

In this context, for men to assert power over women is for them to usurp authority over persons who are their superiors. Marinella describes the relation between men and women as tyrannical; she says that the female sex "is tyrannized and controlled by insolent and unjust men."[238] She treats the power that men exercise over women explicitly as tyrannical throughout the *Nobiltà*, with all the implications that term carries, as suggested by the accounts of Plato and Aristotle: that the power is aimed at satisfying the nonrational desires of men, that a man follows his whims rather than any principle or law, and that the women over whom he exercises power are his equals or superiors.

To make clear that it is the entire male sex that is disposed to tyranny, Marinella contrasts the power that men hold over women to the sort of gentle power (*dolce impero*) that women might exercise over men, writing "But hers [woman's] is a peaceful dominion in line with her nature. For if she lorded over all as a tyrant – as discourteous men do – perhaps then would the insolent detractors of this noble sex be mute,"[239] and "women transform the discourteous man ... ruling him with a gentle dominion, unlike the tyrant's."[240] If the entire female sex is disposed to be gentle and peaceful in the exercise of power, this can be traced to the practical wisdom and the lack of excessive desires, for either pleasure or honor, that characterize the constitution of women, which in turn can be traced to the moderate temperature of the female body.

10 Conclusion

Marinella is remarkable as an early feminist theorist for several features of her work. First, she argues consistently for the unqualified superiority of women over men, in a context in which most pro-woman authors vacillated between claims of equality and claims of superiority. On her account women have nobler souls than men, a physiology better suited to the acquisition of intellectual and moral virtues, and a greater capacity for achieving knowledge of the divine. Second, she builds her arguments by invoking the authority of ancient and contemporary philosophers even as she criticizes, or deviates from, some of their views. That is, she shows exceptional confidence in entering into dialogue with eminent philosophers and positioning herself as their intellectual equal, able to assess their reasoning, and to accept or reject their conclusions. Marinella reveals tensions in their views, and unfounded assumptions and errors of reasoning in their arguments. In doing so she demonstrates her own intellectual authority, and provides us with critical insights into the philosophical underpinnings of Renaissance misogyny. Third, while Marinella's aim is to convince her audience of the worth of women, that aim is not apolitical. Her

---

[238] Marinella, *Nobiltà*, p. 120.   [239] Marinella, *Nobiltà*, p. 12.   [240] Marinella, *Nobiltà*, p. 15.

discussions of topics as distant as the impact of physiology on psychology, the distinctions among virtues and vices, and the nature of liberty all point to a preoccupation with the flawed justifications for the exclusion of women from politics, particularly from political governance, and to an ambition to demonstrate the legitimacy of political rule by women.

Works Cited

Works by Marinella

Marinella, Lucrezia. *Arcadia felice*, ed. F. Lavocat. Florence: Olschki, [1605] 1998.

Marinella, Lucrezia. *De' gesti eroici e della vita meravigliosa della Serafica S. Caterina da Siena*, ed. A. Maggi. Ravenna: Longo, [1624] 2011.

Marinella, Lucrezia. *Enrico; or, Byzantium Conquered: A Heroic Poem*, ed. and trans. M. Galli Stampino. Chicago: University of Chicago Press, 2009.

Marinella, Lucrezia. *L'Enrico, ovvero Bisanzio acquistato, poema eroico*, ed. M. Galli Stampino. Modena: Mucchi, [1635] 2010.

Marinella, Lucrezia. *Exhortations to Women and to Others if They Please*, ed. and trans. Laura Benedetti. Toronto: Centre for Reformation and Renaissance Studies, 2012.

Marinella, Lucrezia. *La nobiltà et l'eccellenza delle donne co' diffetti et mancamenti de gli uomini*. Venice: Giolito, 1601.

Marinella, Lucrezia. *The Nobility and Excellence of Women, and the Defects and Vices of Men*, ed. and trans. Anne Dunhill. Chicago: The University of Chicago Press, 1999.

Other Primary Sources

Agrippa, Henricus Cornelius. *De nobilitate & praecellentia foeminei sexus*. Antwerp: apud Michaelem Hillenium in Rapo, 1529.

Agrippa, Henricus Cornelius. *Declamation on the Nobility and Preeminence of the Female Sex*, ed. and trans. A. Rabil, Jr. Chicago: University of Chicago Press, 1996.

Agrippa, Henricus Cornelius. *Della nobiltà e Eccellenza delle Donne, dalla lingua francese nella italiana tradotto con una Oratione di M. Allessandro Piccolomini in lode delle medesime*, trans. Coccio. Venice: Gabriel Giolito de Ferrari, 1549.

Aristotle. *Generation of Animals*, trans. A. L. Peck. Cambridge, MA: Harvard University Press, 1942.

Aristotle. *Nicomachean Ethics*, trans. C. J. Rowe and S. Broadie. Oxford: Oxford University Press, 2002.

Aristotle. *Parts of Animals*, trans. J. G. Lennox. Oxford: Oxford University Press, 2001.

Aristotle. *Politics*, trans. C. Lord, 2nd ed. Chicago: Chicago University Press, 2013.

Aristotle. *The Complete Works*, ed. J. Barnes. Princeton: Princeton University Press, 1984.

Bronzino, Cristoforo. *Della dignità e nobiltà delle donne: Dialogo di Cristofano Bronzini* [sic], *diviso in quattro settimane, e ciascheduna di esse in sei giornate*. Florence: Zanobi Pignoni, 1622.

Bruni, Leonardo. *Politicorum libri VIII latine ex versione Leonardi Aretini*. Rome: E. Silber, 1492.

Capella (Capra), Galeazzo Flavio. *Della eccellenza et dignità delle donne*, ed. M. L. Doglio. 2nd ed. Rome: Bulzoni Editore, [1525] 2001.

Castiglione, Baldassare. *Il Libro del cortegiano*, ed. Ettore Bonora. Milan: Mursia, 1972.

Castiglione, Baldassare. *Il Cortegiano di Baldessare Castiglione*, trans. and eds. A. Busi and C. Covito. Milan: Rizzoli, 1993.

Castiglione, Baldassare. *The Book of the Courtier*, trans. Charles S. Singleton. New York: Doubleday, 1959.

Dante (Alighieri, Dante). *Convivio: A Dual-Language Critical Edition*, ed. and trans. Andrew Frisardi. Cambridge: Cambridge University Press, 2018.

Domenichi, Lodovico. *La nobiltà delle donne*. Venice: Giolito, 1549/1551.

Ficino, Marsilio. *Commentaire sur le banquet de Platon*, ed. and trans. Raymond Marcel. Paris: Les belles lettres, 1956.

Ficino, Marsilio. *Commentary on Plato's Symposium*, trans. and intro. Sears Reynolds Jayne. Columbia: University of Missouri, 1944.

Hippocrates. *Oeuvres complètes d' Hippocrate*, trans. and ed. E. Littré. Paris: J. B. Baillière, 1839–61.

Machiavelli, Niccolò. *Discourses on the First Ten Books of Titus Livius*, trans. C. E. Detmold. New York: Modern Library, 1950.

Maggi, Vincenzo. *Un brieve trattato dell'eccellentia delle donne*. Brescia: Damiano de Turlini, 1545.

Naugerius, Andreas. *Andreae Naugerii: Opera Omnia*, ed. J. A. Vulpius. Padova: Cominus, 1718.

Passi, Giuseppe. *I donneschi difetti*. Venice: Giovanni Antonio Somasco, 1599.

de Pizan, Christine. *Debate of the "Romance of the Rose,"* ed. and trans. David F. Hult. Chicago: University of Chicago Press, 2010.

Plato. *Complete Works*, ed. J. M. Cooper. Indianapolis, IN: Hackett, 1997.

Plotinus. *The Essential Plotinus: Representative Treatises from the Enneads*, trans. E. J. O'Brien. Indianapolis, IN: Hackett, 1964.

Plutarch. *Moralia*, trans. Frank Cole Babbitt. Cambridge, MA: Harvard University Press, 1968.

Tasso, Torquato. *Discorso della virtù feminile e donnesca*, ed. M. L. Doglio. Palermo: Sellerio Editore, [1582] 1997.

Secondary Sources

Angenot, Marc. *Les Champions des femmes: examen du discours sur la supériorité des femmes, 1400–1800*. Montreal: Presses de l'Université du Québec, 1977.

Bayle, Pierre. *Dictionnaire historique et critique*, 3rd ed. Rotterdam: Michel Bohm, 1720.

Benedetti, Laura. "Arcangela Tarabotti e Lucrezia Marinella: Appunti per un dialogo mancato," *Modern Language Notes* 129 (3S) (2014), 87–97.

Benedetti, Laura. "Le *Essortationi* di Lucrezia Marinella: L'ultimo messaggio di una misteriosa Veneziana," *Italica* 85 (4) (2008), 381–395.

Bolufer, Mónica. "Medicine and the *Querelle des Femmes* in Early Modern Spain," *Medical History* 29 (2009), 86–106.

Bouwsma, William J. *Venice and the Defense of Republican Liberty*. Berkeley: University of California Press, 1968.

Cadden, Joan. *Meanings of Sex Difference in the Middle Ages: Medicine, Science, and Culture*. Cambridge: Cambridge University Press, 1993.

Cagnolati, Antonella. "Un duello in punta di penna: Strategie antimisogine nella *Nobiltà*." In Antonella Cagnolati (ed.), *A Portrait of a Renaissance Feminist: Lucrezia Marinella's Life and Works*. Rome: Aracne, 2013, 41–66.

Chemello, Adriana. "La donna, il modello, l'immaginario: Moderata Fonte e Lucrezia Marinella." In Marina Zancan (ed.), *Nel cerchio della luna: Figure di donna in alcuni testi del XVI secolo*. Venice: Marsilio, 1983, 95–170.

Chiappini, Luciano. *Eleanora d'Aragona, prima Duchessa di Ferrara*. Rovigo: S.T.E.R., 1956.

Cox, Virginia. "Gender and Eloquence in Ercole de' Roberti's *Portia and Brutus* ," *Renaissance Quarterly* 62 (2009), 60–101.

Cox, Virginia. "Members, Muses, and Mascots: Women and the Italian Academies." In Jane Everson, Denis V. Reidy, and Lisa Sampson, (eds.), *The Italian Academies, 1525–1700: Networks of Culture, Innovation, and Dissent*. Cambridge and Abingdon: MHRA and Routledge, 2016, 132–167.

Cox, Virginia. *The Prodigious Muse: Women's Writing in Counter-Reformation Italy*. Baltimore: The Johns Hopkins University Press, 2011.

Cox, Virginia. "The Single Self: Feminist Thought and the Marriage Market in Early Modern Venice," *Renaissance Quarterly* XLVIII (1995), 513–581.

Cox, Virginia. *Women's Writing in Italy*. Baltimore: The Johns Hopkins University Press, 2008.

Crawford, K. "Marsilio Ficino, Neoplatonism, and the Problem of Sex," *Renaissance and Reformation*, 28 (2) (Spring 2004), 3–35.

Daenens, Francine. "Superiore perché inferior: il paradosso della superiorità in alcuni trattati italiani del Cinquecento." In V. Gentili, (ed.), *Trasgressione tragica e norma domestica*. Rome: Edizioni di storia e letteratura, 1983, 11–50.

Deslauriers, Marguerite. "Marinella and Her Interlocutors: Hot Blood, Hot Words, Hot Deeds," *Philosophical Studies* 174 (10) (2017), 2525–2537. http://link.springer.com/article/10.1007/s11098-016-0730-3.

Deslauriers, Marguerite. "Political Rule over Women in *Politics* I." In T. Lockwood and T. Samaras, (eds.), *Aristotle's* Politics: *A Critical Guide*. Cambridge: Cambridge University Press, 2015, 55–75.

Deslauriers, Marguerite. "The Conceptualization of Masculine Authority as Unjust: Tyranny in 17th Century Venice," *British Journal for the History of Philosophy*, 27 (4) (2019), 718–737. DOI: https://doi.org/10.1080/09608788.2018.1537256.

Deslauriers, Marguerite. "The Superiority of Seventeenth Century Women," *Journal of the American Philosophical Association*, July 1–19, 2021. DOI: https://doi.org/10.1017/apa.2019.24.

Dialeti, Androniki. "A Woman Defending Women: Breaking with Tradition in Lucrezia Marinella's *La nobiltà, et eccellenze delle donne*." In Antonella Cagnolati (ed.), *A Portrait of a Renaissance Feminist: Lucrezia Marinella's Life and Works*. Rome: Aracne, 2013, 67–104.

Ducharme, Isabelle. "Marguerite Buffet: lectrice de la Querelle des femmes." In I. Brouard-Arends (ed.), *Lectrices d'ancien régime*. Rennes: Presses Universitaires de Rennes, 2003, 311–320.

Firenzuola, Agnolo. *On the Beauty of Women*, K. Eisenbichler, and J. Murray (trans. and eds.). Philadelphia: University of Pennsylvania Press, 1992.

Galen. *Works on Human Nature*, Vol. 1 *Mixtures* (*De Temperamentis*), P. N. Singer and Philip J. van der Eijk (eds. and trans.). Cambridge: Cambridge University Press, 2018.

Gerson, Lloyd. "Plotinus," *The Stanford Encyclopedia of Philosophy* (Fall 2018 Edition), Edward N. Zalta (ed.), https://plato.stanford.edu/archives/fall2018/entries/plotinus.

Gilbert, Felix. "The Venetian Constitution in Florentine Political Thought." In Nicolai Rubinstein (ed.), *Florentine Studies: Politics and Society in Renaissance Florence*, London: Faber and Faber, 1968, 463–500.

Gogol, Ryan. "The Literary Exchange between Lucrezia Marinella and Cristofano Bronzini." In Marinella, L., *De' gesti eroici e della vita meravigliosa della Serafica S. Caterina da Siena*, A. Maggi (ed.). Ravenna: Longo, 2011, 213–228.

Hankins, James. *Plato in the Italian Renaissance*. Leiden: Brill, 1990.

Haskins, Susan. "A Portrait." In Antonella Cagnolati (ed.), *A Portrait of a Renaissance Feminist: Lucrezia Marinella's Life and Works*. Rome: Aracne, 2013, 11–40.

Haskins, Susan. "Vexatious Litigant, or the Case of Lucrezia Marinella? New Documents Concerning Her Life (Part I)." *Nouvelles de la République des Lettres* 1 (2006), 80–128.

Haskins, Susan. "Vexatious Litigant, or the Case of Lucrezia Marinella? New Documents Concerning Her Life (Part II)." *Nouvelles de la République des Lettres* 1–2 (2007), 203–230.

Hult, David F. "The *Roman de la rose*, Christine de Pizan, and the *querelle des femmes*." In Carolyn Dinshaw and David Wallace (eds.), *The Cambridge Companion to Medieval Women's Writing*. Cambridge: Cambridge University Press, 2003, 184–194.

James, Carolyn. "Margherita Cantelmo and the Worth of Women in Renaissance Italy." In Karen Green and Constant Mews (eds.), *Virtue Ethics for Women 1250-1500*. Dordrecht: Springer Netherlands, 2011, 145–163.

Jordan, Constance. *Renaissance Feminism: Literary Texts and Political Models*. Ithaca, NY: Cornell University Press, 1990.

Jouanna, Jacques. *Greek Medicine from Hippocrates to Galen: Selected Papers*, Philip van der Eijk (ed.), Neil Allies (trans.). Leiden: Brill, 2012.

Kelly, Joan. "Early Feminist Theory and the 'Querelle des Femmes,' 1400–1789." *Signs* 8 (1) (1982), 4–28.

King, Helen. *Hippocrates' Woman: Reading the Female Body in Ancient Greece*. New York: Routledge, 1998.

King, Margaret L. "A Return to the Ancient World?" In *The Oxford Handbook of Early Modern European History*. Oxford: Oxford University Press, 2015, 3–28.

King, Margaret L. "Six Learned Women of the Italian Renaissance," *Soundings: An Interdisciplinary Journal* 59:3 (Fall 1976), 280–304.

Kolsky, Stephen. "Moderata Fonte, Lucrezia Marinella, Giuseppe Passi: An Early Seventeenth-Century Feminist Controversy." *The Modern Language Review* 96 (4) (2001): 973–989.

Kolsky, Stephen. *The Ghost of Boccaccio: Writings on Famous Women in Renaissance Italy*. Turnhout: Brepols Publishers, 2005.

Kolsky, Stephen. "The Literary Career of Lucrezia Marinella (1571–1653)." In F. W. Kent & C. Zika (eds.), *Rituals, Images, and Words: Varieties of Cultural Expression in Late Medieval and Early Modern Europe*. Turnhout: Brepols, 2005, 325–342.

Lane, Frederic C. "At the Roots of Republicanism," *The American Historical Review* 71: 2 (1966), 403–420.

Langlands, Rebecca. "Lucrezia Marinella's Feminism and the Authority of the Classics," unpublished paper, 1995.

Lavocat, Françoise. "Introduzione." In Marinella, Lucrezia, *Arcadia felice*. Florence: Olschki, 1998, vii–lx.

Leunissen, Mariska. *From Natural Character to Moral Virtue in Aristotle*. Oxford: Oxford University Press, 2017.

Lévêque, P. *Aurea catena Homeri: une etude sur l'allégorie Grecque: Annales Littéraires De L'université De Besancon*, Vol. 27. Paris: Les Belles Lettres, 1959.

Libby, Lester J. "Venetian History and Political Thought after 1509." *Studies in the Renaissance* 20 (1973), 7–45.

Lorenz, Hendrik. *The Brute Within: Appetitive Desire in Plato and Aristotle*. Oxford: Clarendon, 2006.

Lovejoy, Arthur O. *The Great Chain of Being*. Cambridge, MA: Harvard University Press, 1936.

Maclean, Ian. *The Renaissance Notion of Woman: A Study in the Fortunes of Scholasticism and Medical Science in European Intellectual Life*. Cambridge: Cambridge University Press, 1980.

Maggi, Vincenzo. *Un brieve trattato dell'eccellentia delle donne*. In Sandra Plastina, *Mollezza della carne e sotigliezza dell'ingegno: la natura della donna nel Rinascimento europeo*. Rome: Carocci, 2017, 147–162.

Malpezzi Price, Paola and Ristaino, Christine. *Lucrezia Marinella and the "Querelle Des Femmes" in Seventeenth-Century Italy*. Madison: Fairleigh Dickinson University Press, 2008.

Manca, Joseph. "'Constantia et Forteza': Eleanora d'Aragona's Famous Matrons." *Source: Notes in the History of Art*, 19:2, 2000, 13–20.

Mazzeo, Joseph Anthony. "The Augustinian Conception of Beauty and Dante's *Convivio*." *The Journal of Aesthetics and Art Criticism*, 15:4 (June 1957), 435–448.

McWebb, C. *Debating the Roman de la Rose: A Critical Anthology*. New York: Routledge, 2007.

Moss, Jessica. "Appearances and Calculations: Plato's Division of the Soul." *Oxford Studies in Ancient Philosophy*, 34 (2008), 35–68.

Nutton, Vivian. "God, Galen and the Depaganization of Ancient Medicine." In P. Biller and J. Ziegler (eds.), *Religion and Medicine in the Middle Ages.* York: York Medieval Press, 2001, 17–32.

Panizza, Letizia. "Introduction." In Anne Dunhill (ed. and trans.), *Lucrezia Marinella: The Nobility and Excellence of Women and the Defects and Vices of Men.* Chicago: University of Chicago Press, 1999.

Panizza, Letizia. "Introduction." In Arcangela Tarabotti, *Paternal Tyranny,* Letizia Panizza (trans. and ed.). Chicago: University of Chicago Press, 2004, 1–32.

Panizza, Letizia. "Platonic Love on the Rocks: Castiglione Counter-Currents in Renaissance Italy." In Stephen Clucas, Peter J. Forshaw, and Valery Rees (eds.), *Laus Platonici Philosophi.* Leiden: Brill, 2011, 199–226.

Parry, John J. "Introduction" in Andreas Cappellanus, *The Art of Courtly Love.* New York: Columbia University Press, 1960, 3–24.

Piana, Marco. "Divinae Pulchritudinis Imago: The Neoplatonic Construction of Female Identity in Lucrezia Marinella's *La nobiltà et l'eccellenze delle donne* (1601)." In S. Santosuosso (ed.), *Genealogie. Re-Writing the Canon: Women Writing in XVI–XVII Century Italy.* Seville: Arcibel Editores, 2018, 199–221.

Pomata, Gianna. "Was There a Querelle des femmes in Early Modern Medicine?" *Arenal: Revista de Historia de las Mujeres,* 20 (3) (2013), 213–241.

Ray, Meredith K. *Daughters of Alchemy: Women and Scientific Culture in Early Modern Italy.* Cambridge, MA: Harvard University Press, 2015.

Rich, Audrey N. M. "The Platonic Ideas as the Thoughts of God," *Mnemosyne,* Fourth Series 7:2 (1954), 123–133.

Ross, Sarah Gwyneth. *The Birth of Feminism: Woman as Intellect in Renaissance Italy and England.* Cambridge, MA: Harvard University Press, 2009.

Rubinstein, Nicolai. "Political Ideas in Sienese Art: The Frescoes by Ambrogio Lorenzetti and Taddeo di Bartolo in the Palazzo Pubblico." *Journal of the Warburg and Courtauld Institutes* 21:3/4 (1958), 179–207.

Schmitt, Charles B. *Aristotle and the Renaissance.* Cambridge, MA: Harvard University Press, 1983.

Shapiro, Lisa. "The Outward and Inward Beauty of Early Modern Women." *Revue Philosophique de La France et de l'Étranger* 203:3 (2013), 327–346.

Sinclair, Amy. "Latin in Lucrezia Marinella's *Essortationi alle donne* (1645): Subverting the Voice of Authority." In Del Soldato, E. and Rizzi, A. (eds.),

City, Court, Academy: Language Choice in Early Modern Italy. London: Routledge, 2017, 117–134.

Weaver, Elissa B., "Introduction" in Arcangela Tarabotti, *Antisatire: In Defense of Women, against Franceco Buoninsegni*, E. B. Weaver (ed. and trans.). New York/Toronto: Iter Press, 2020.

Willer, Annika. "Silent Deletions: The Two Different Editions of Lucrezia Marinella's *La Nobiltà et l'eccellenza delle donne*," *Bruniana e campanelliana: ricerche filosofiche e materiali storico-testuali*, 19:1 (2013), 207–219.

Zonta, G. *Trattati del Cinquecento sulla donna*. Bari: Laterza,1913.

Acknowledgments

This *Element* draws on research supported by the Social Sciences and Humanities Research Council of Canada. I wish to thank the Biblioteca Aprosiana in Ventimiglia, and the librarian there, Giovanni Russo, for granting me access to an early edition of Marinella's *Essortationi* and for illuminating how and when it was acquired. I would also like to acknowledge the assistance of the staff at the Archivio di Stato in Modena in interpreting Marinella's handwriting, and of the staff at the Biblioteca Estense Universitaria in finding materials. I am grateful for their patience and expertise. Lara Harwood-Ventura provided invaluable help on philological and historical questions. Decio Cusmano offered impeccable editorial assistance in the final stages; remaining errors are, of course, mine. I would also like to acknowledge the insights and suggestions of the participants in a Journal of the History of Philosophy Summer Seminar on Lucrezia Marinella that I led at McGill University in May 2022: Olivia Branscum, Allauren Forbes, Ronja Hildebrandt, Hannah Laurens, Margaret Matthews, and Simona Vucu. It was a real pleasure for me to think through Marinella's arguments with them. Finally, I am grateful to my colleagues in the *Extending New Narratives* network of researchers for intellectual exchanges and encouragement, especially Sandrine Bergès, Jacqueline Broad, Martina Reuter, and Lisa Shapiro.

For Kim Turner and Siân Evans, first feminists

Cambridge Elements ≡

Women in the History of Philosophy

Jacqueline Broad

Monash University

Jacqueline Broad is Professor of Philosophy at Monash University, Australia. Her area of expertise is early modern philosophy, with a special focus on seventeenth and eighteenth-century women philosophers. She is the author of *Women Philosophers of the Seventeenth Century* (Cambridge University Press, 2002), *A History of Women's Political Thought in Europe, 1400–1700* (with Karen Green; Cambridge University Press, 2009), and *The Philosophy of Mary Astell: An Early Modern Theory of Virtue* (Oxford University Press, 2015).

Advisory Board

About the Series

In this Cambridge Elements series, distinguished authors provide concise and structured introductions to a comprehensive range of prominent and lesser-known figures in the history of women's philosophical endeavour, from ancient times to the present day.

Printed in the United States
by Baker & Taylor Publisher Services